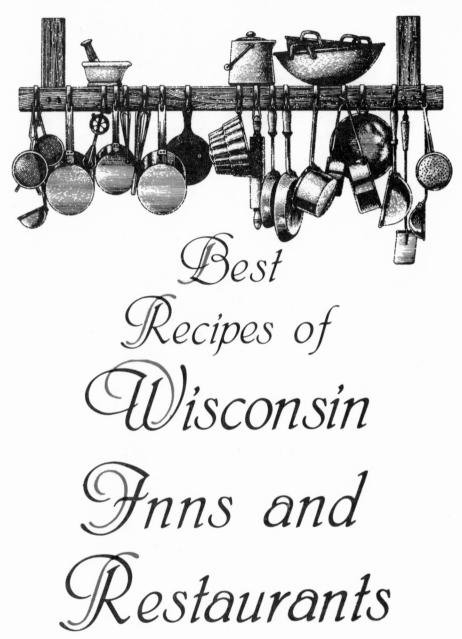

Best Recipes of Wisconsin Inns and Restaurants

Compiled and edited by:
Margaret E. Guthrie

Editorial assistance:
Rosemarie Putman

First edition, third printing (revised).

Library of Congress Catalog Number: 86-61171

ISBN: 0-910122-87-3

For additional copies of this book, contact:

Amherst Press
A division of Palmer Publications, Inc.
P.O. Box 296
Amherst, Wisconsin 54406

Table of Contents

Preface IV

Introduction V

Brunch 1

Bread, Rolls, Muffins 17

Appetizers 29

Soups 39

Meat & Poultry 53

Fish & Seafood 75

Salads & Salad Dressings 85

Desserts 99

Inns & Restaurants 123

Index 126

Preface

Once upon a time it was customary to say grace before a meal, to at least acknowledge that the food was there because of others than those at the table.

Before we get to the food in this book, I would like to acknowledge the people who helped me to make it happen. First, there is the publisher and my good friend, Chuck Spanbauer, who spent five years of his life working with me and still had faith in me and this idea of mine. He is as big a foodie as I am.

There is my friend, Stephen Herzberg, as entertaining and appreciative a dinner companion as one could ask for, who began the Milwaukee list for me. There are many restaurant owners, managers and chefs who were cooperative, appreciative and who tipped me off to others. Kevin McCarty of the White Gull Inn and Nancy Christy of Chez Michel are two that were particularly helpful.

My attorney, Michael R. Davis, who crossed all the t's and dotted all the i's, making it smooth sailing. Friends and acquaintances who told me about restaurants that had to be included. Finally, there are my three children whose senses of humor rescued me more than once.

Thank you all. Bon Appetit.

Introduction

When I first moved to Wisconsin nine years ago I knew very little about the state. I knew that Wisconsin had been the major beer brewing state. I knew that the Green Bay Packers lived here, that the Milwaukee Brewers were based here, and that it was America's Dairyland. The license plates told me so.

On my way to Wisconsin from New England I stopped to visit my parents. My father told me that Wisconsin was one of the most beautiful of the 48 contiguous states. Since he had been in all of them, I felt sure he was a good judge and he was.

What disappointed me at first, though, was the food. It seemed to me that Wisconsin deserved its reputation as a beer and bratwurst sort of place. There's nothing wrong with either good beer or good bratwurst, just that as a diet it lacks variety.

As I moved around the state and began to write about food and restaurants, I realized just how wrong I had been. I also realized that many other people had the same impression.

The idea for this book came from that realization and the realization that although Wisconsin enjoys a hearty tourist business, there is no overall book about its restaurants, its foods. There was nothing to tell you where to go to eat what.

This book is a modest attempt to give people an idea of what is available in restaurants around the state. If there seems to be more in the book from the southeastern part of the state, that's because there are more people living there and as a result, more restaurants.

As we talked to chefs, restaurant managers and owners around the state, we found that there is a deep appreciation for the local foods. You will find recipes in the book for morels, chèvre frais, wild fruits, even crawfish, as well as veal, duckling and many of the more "ordinary" products of Wisconsin's widely varied agriculture.

We'd like to share with you what one chef had to say when he submitted his recipes:

"The ingredients available in northern France (the area around Normandy in particular) are remarkably similar in variety and quality to those available in Wisconsin. Our best butter, cream, beef, pork, apples, squash and native and transplanted fish (lake trout, coho salmon, etc.) compare favorably to their French counterparts. We are fortunate to have morels, wild strawberries, blackberries, etc. that are bountiful in Wisconsin and rare in other states. A new breed of 'farmer' is emerging and it is now possible to obtain fresh herbs, goat cheeses, ciders, and berries that hold their own in any comparison . . ."

You will also find that Wisconsin's chefs and cooks are up on all the latest in cuisine and food trends. One of the contributing chefs was selected by "Food and

Wine" magazine as one of the twenty-five outstanding young chefs in America today.

A certain sophistication has come to the small, out-of-the-way restaurants, too. You will find recipes for moussaka, Cajun specialities and quiches from restaurants all around the state, rather than in just the large metropolitan areas.

Wisconsin's chefs take having all that coastline seriously. You will find many recipes for fish and seafood. These are newly popular because we are all more health conscious and because air freight has brought us truly fresh fish from the ocean.

Soup seemed to be a very popular recipe to submit, perhaps giving a clue to our climate. Pie was another big favorite. We could almost do a whole book on Wisconsin pies. Chocolate is as popular in Wisconsin as it is anywhere.

Since we set out to show the variety and diversity of Wisconsin food and cooking, we have left the recipes very much as the chefs wrote them. Some of the chefs asked us to tell readers to be sure and use the ingredients designated and not to substitute, if desired results are to be achieved.

If your favorite restaurant is missing from our book, we apologize. We did try to find them all, some chose not to participate and I'm sure that we have missed a few.

Brunch

Brunch

Brunch, that meal that is usually served mid to late morning and whose etymology is the combination of breakfast and lunch, has become very popular. Perhaps because of the large increase of women in the work force or the hectic pace of our lives; for whatever reasons, we are now offered wonderful brunches by restaurants everywhere. When the food is as terrific as some of the recipes here, who cares why as much as how. So, here's how, if you'd like some ideas for serving your own brunch.

Our brunch offers everything from special pancakes to make-from-scratch ravioli. There are special sauces, some adaptable to pasta, rice or crepes, unusual sandwiches and an authentic Cornish pasty. There are eggs and abelskivers for the breakfast side of brunch, moussaka and ciociara sauce for the luncheon side of brunch.

Sunrise Buttermilk Pancakes

A Northwoods daybreak tradition. Wild blueberries added to the batter make a great flavor enhancer!

2 fresh, large eggs
¼ cup brown sugar
1½ tsps. salt
3 Tbsps. melted butter
1 Tbsp. baking powder
2 cups fresh buttermilk*
2 cups white flour
1 tsp. baking soda

Beat eggs until light and frothy. Add brown sugar, salt, melted butter and buttermilk. Mix until combined. Add flour, soda, and baking powder. Beat until batter is smooth.

Drop ¼ to ½ cup batter (depending on desired size) onto griddle. Flip after bubbles appear on top and bottoms are golden. Remove from griddle when firm and bottoms are brown. Serve immediately with Wisconsin butter and 100% maple syrup. Yield: Serves 4-5 persons.

*Buttermilk consistency varies. If batter is too thick increase buttermilk slightly.

From: **The Sunrise Lodge**
Land O'Lakes, Wisconsin

Abelskivers

3 eggs
2 cups buttermilk
1 tsp. baking soda
½ Tbsp. sugar
2 cups flour
1 tsp. baking powder
½ tsp. salt
chopped apples to taste

Separate eggs, beat whites, set aside. Beat yolks, add other ingredients. Add egg whites last. Fold together. Be sure Abelskiver iron is hot and holes are half full of oil. Put a heaping spoon of batter in each hole. Add a piece of apple, prune or a little jam to each. Turn with a long slender knitting needle. Keep turning until golden brown all over. Drain, sprinkle with powdered sugar and serve.

Please note: If the pan is too hot, skivers will burn before they are fully cooked.

From: **The Summer Kitchen**
Ephraim, Wisconsin

Jack Pandl's Famous German Pancake

½ cup white flour
½ cup milk
pinch of salt
4 large eggs
1 Tbsp. butter
1 Tbsp. shortening
lemon wedges
maple syrup
powdered sugar
butter

Mix the flour, milk, and salt together in a mixing bowl until smooth. Add the eggs and beat until smooth.

Preheat oven to 425 degrees.

Melt the butter and shortening in a 9" or 10" slope sided pan with an ovenproof handle. Pour the batter into the pan and cook on the stove until the bottom of the pancake is browned, but uncooked batter remains on top, about 2-3 minutes.

With a spatula, turn the pancake quickly and make a crisscross cut all the way through the pancake. Put in preheated oven about 12 minutes or until the edges are browned. The pancake will rise 3"-5" all around the edges of the pan. The criss-cross will close as the pancake bakes.

Remove the pancake from the oven and quickly cut into 6 servings. Serve immediately with lemon, 100% maple syrup, powdered sugar and butter.

From:

**Jack Pandl's
Whitefish Bay Inn**
1319 East Henry Clay Road
Whitefish Bay, Wisconsin

Cornish Pasty

3 lbs. round steak, cubed
4 cups potatoes, thinly sliced
ground suet
1 cup rutabagas, thinly sliced
1½ cups chopped onions
salt & pepper to taste
butter

Roll out dough as for pie crust. Place mixture of meat, vegetables and fat on half of crust. Fold over the other half on top and seal edge, crimping with fork or fingers. Bake at 350 degrees for 1½ hours. This may also be baked in a 9" x 13" pan for 3 hours, covering the top crust with foil for the first two hours of baking.

Pasty Crust:
4 cups flour
½ tsp. baking powder
cold water enough to make pastry
1 cup lard
¼ tsp. salt

Mix lard into flour, baking powder and salt as you would for pie crust. Add enough water to make pastry. Roll out. Yield: 6 to 8 individual pasties, or one 9" x 13" pan.

From: **The Red Rooster Cafe**
Mineral Point, Wisconsin

HiFi Sandwich

Our high fiber sandwich is very popular.

firm bodied whole wheat bread
butter
raisins
leaf lettuce
natural chunky peanut butter

Spread butter on two slices of bread. Spread peanut butter on one slice and mayonnaise on the other. Sprinkle a tablespoon of raisins on the peanut butter. Spread a handful of grated carrot on the raisins. Top

mayonnaise
shredded carrots

the carrots with a crisp lettuce leaf. Put the other slice of bread on top. Cut in half and enjoy. You now have a well-balanced meal.

From: **The Summer Kitchen**
Ephraim, Wisconsin

Jane's Mexican Quiche

In a single pie shell, unbaked:

cream cheese or grated Cheddar
refried beans or
  browned hamburger
green pepper
fresh mushrooms
onion
cumin
chili powder
hot sauce
black olives
3 eggs
1 cup milk
grated Cheddar cheese
chives

Layer bottom of pie shell with cream cheese or grated Cheddar. Next layer refried beans or hamburger. Saute green pepper, mushrooms and onions together with a dash of cumin, chili powder for next layer. Add hot sauce to taste and black olives. Mix three eggs and milk and pour over all. Top with grated Cheddar cheese and chives. Bake at 350 degrees for 45 minutes.

From: **The Mill Road Cafe**
Mill Road
Galesville, Wisconsin

Kitchen Scrambler

Ambrosia! Vary amount for the number of people and appetites.

butter
onions, diced
chives
peas, fresh or frozen
alfalfa sprouts
eggs
natural Cheddar cheese,
  shredded
tomatoes, diced

Saute onions, peas and chives in butter. Lightly beat eggs with a granny fork. Pour into sauteed vegetables. Lightly scramble eggs and vegetables. Move batter around in pan with granny fork as the eggs congeal so that the final product is not a solid mass.

Remove from heat. Cover with Cheddar cheese, put lid on pan for about 15 seconds to let cheese melt. Remove eggs to a warm plate, topped with diced tomatoes and sprouts.

Serve with toasted wheat bread and country fries.

Country Fries

potatoes, scrubbed
fat

Cut potatoes into any shape, leaving skins on. Put in a skillet with hot fat, or electric skillet turned to 375 degrees. Fry until a golden brown.

Delicious! No additives.

From: **The Summer Kitchen**
Ephraim, Wisconsin

Ravioli

Filling:
1 pint of ricotta cheese
½ cup imported Parmesan cheese,
   grated
3 large fresh parsley springs
2 large eggs
½ cup Mozzarella cheese, grated
garlic salt

Blend all ingredients together.

Pasta Dough:
3 large eggs
2 Tbsps. olive oil
3 cups cold mashed potatoes
4 cups flour
1 tsp. salt

Blend eggs, oil, potatoes and salt thoroughly. Add flour sparingly until dough is ready to knead, adding flour as needed. Roll out dough ¹/₁₆", cut in 5" circles. Place spoonful of filling in center of circles, fold and crimp to seal.

These can be frozen or refrigerated until ready to use.

Boil for fifteen minutes in your favorite tomato sauce.

From: **Peck's Plantation**
Hwy. 73 East
Wautoma, Wisconsin

Pesto Pasta

4 cloves garlic, diced
olive oil
1 bunch chopped, fresh parsley
3 Tbsps. flaked sweet basil**
3 Tbsps. Romano cheese
½ tsp. salt
½ tsp. pepper

Put diced garlic in blender, add ¼ cup olive oil, and liquefy. Add chopped parsley and ¼ cup olive oil, liquefy. Add basil, cheese, salt & pepper plus ½ cup olive oil until completely liquefied.

Pesto is added to any cooked and drained pasta. Pasta and Pesto mix must be stirred vigorously, so we recommend a flat cake pan for mixing.

*Note: When draining pasta, save the water. Add some of the pasta water back when mixing in Pesto mix. This will impart flavor. Pesto Pasta should be juicy. At the Granary we use an imported fettucini.

**Note: When available, use fresh sweet basil, increasing amount to taste.

From: **The Granary**
50 West 6th Avenue
Oshkosh, Wisconsin

Ciociara Sauce
(For Pasta, Rice, or Crepes)

3 Tbsps. unsalted butter
2 Tbsps. flour
3 Tbsps. olive oil
¼ cup minced onion
2 Tbsps. grated carrot

Make a roux by melting 2 tablespoons of the butter in a saucepan. Stir in the flour and mix until well incorporated. Cook over low heat, stirring often for 5 minutes. Remove from heat and set aside.

1 bay leaf
1 Tbsp. lemon zest
⅓ cup brandy
¾ cup bottled clam juice
1 cup peeled, chopped,
   fresh tomato
¾ cup heavy cream
¼ tsp. black pepper
1½ lbs. shrimp or favorite seafood

Heat the remaining butter and olive oil in a heavy saucepan and saute the onion, carrot, bay leaf and the lemon zest. Cook, stirring often, for 10 minutes.

Pour the brandy over the ingredients and set aflame.

When the flames die, add all of the remaining ingredients except the seafood. Heat about 5 minutes, until you have a nice simmer.

Add the roux, stir until the mixture thickens, about 5-10 minutes.

Add the seafood and cook over low heat until the seafood is just cooked through and tender. Add salt to taste and serve. Yield: 4-6 servings.

From: **The Ovens of Brittany
—East**
1718 Fordem Road
Madison, Wisconsin

Spaghetti Sauce

1 lb. ground beef
2 Tbsps. salt
1 Tbsp. pepper
1 Tbsp. garlic powder
1 large onion
5 cloves garlic, finely chopped
1 Tbsp. sweet basil
½ tsp. onion salt
¼ cup chopped parsley
½ tsp. garlic salt
5 32-oz. cans whole tomatoes
1 32-oz. can tomato paste

Brown ground beef with first nine items. Then add 5 cans whole tomatoes, chopped. Last add the tomato paste. Bring to a boil and simmer for 2 hours.

From: **Peck's Plantation**
Hwy. 73 East
Wautoma, Wisconsin

Moussaka

1½ lbs. ground lamb
  browned and drained
2 eggplants, peeled, sliced,
  ½" thick
2 onions, finely chopped
3 Tbsps. tomato paste
¼ cup butter
4 Tbsps. dry red wine
4 Tbsps. parsley, chopped
⅛ tsp. cinnamon
salt & pepper to taste

4 Tbsps. butter
3-4 Tbsps. flour
2 cups milk, scalded

2 eggs, beaten
1 cup ricotta or cottage cheese
⅛ tsp. nutmeg

½ cup fine bread crumbs
½ cup Parmesan cheese

Brown eggplant in 2 tablespoons of butter. In the same skillet, brown onions, add meat and cook for 5 minutes.

Separately combine the tomato paste, butter, wine, parsley, cinnamon, salt and pepper. Add to meat and onion mixture and simmer until all liquid is absorbed.

Make the white sauce—melt butter, add flour, cook over low heat for 3-4 minutes. Add milk slowly, stirring constantly. When thick and smooth, remove from heat. When slightly cool, add eggs, nutmeg and ricotta.

Lightly grease a 9" x 12" pan, sprinkle the bottom with bread crumbs. Arrange eggplant and meat sauce in layers, sprinkling each layer with bread crumbs and Parmesan cheese. Pour cheese sauce over the top and bake in 350 degree oven for one hour or until golden brown.

Remove from oven and cool to allow moussaka to set up. Cut into squares and serve.

May be made a day in advance and reheated or served at room temperature. Yield: 4-5 servings.

From: **The Prairieland Cafe**
137 Albany Street
Spring Green, Wisconsin

Potato Zucchini Pancakes

½ lb. zucchini
1¾ lbs. baking potatoes
1 small onion
3 eggs
oil
½ cup flour
½ cup cornmeal
1 Tbsp. salt
½ tsp. black pepper

Scrub zucchini and potatoes thoroughly. Grate them in food processor or by hand. With a clean, dry towel, squeeze out as much liquid as possible from the grated potatoes and zucchini.

Mince or grate onion.

Beat eggs in large bowl. Add potatoes, zucchini, onion, flour, cornmeal, salt and pepper. Mix well. Mixture should hold together easily.

Cover bottom of flat bottomed heavy skillet with cooking oil. Heat oil until very hot. Add a scoop of the potato mixture to the hot oil and flatten quickly with a spatula or spoon. Continue with more scoops of the mixture until the pan is filled, but not crowded. Fry them on fairly high heat until golden brown on both sides. If pan starts to smoke, lower the flame. Drain cooked pancakes on paper towels. Repeat this process until all the potato mixture is used up, using more oil as required. Serve this pancake with maple syrup, sour cream or a fresh fruit sauce.

From: **The Ovens of Brittany —East**
1718 Fordem Road
Madison, Wisconsin

Garden Vegetable Dish

8 slices bread, cubed
1 lb. breakfast sausage,
  ham, or bacon,
  whichever preferred, diced
2 Tbsps. onion, finely chopped
3 Tbsps. green pepper,
  finely chopped
1 cup broccoli
1 dozen large eggs
1 cup hot water, with 2 Tbsps.
  chicken bouillon, dissolved
1 cup milk
¼ tsp. black pepper
½ tsp. onion powder
1 Tbsp. parsley, finely chopped
2 cans cream of chicken soup
4 large red tomatoes, sliced thin
2 cups shredded Cheddar cheese

Cover the bottom of a 9″ x 13″ pan with cubed bread. Then layer on diced meat, onion, pepper and broccoli. Mix eggs, water, milk and seasonings, mix in soup and pour over top.

Lay tomato slices on top, cover with the shredded cheese.

You may use anything from olives to spinach in place of any or all of the given vegetables. Let stand overnight.

Bake at 325 degrees for about 35 minutes or until firm. Cut into 2″ pieces and let cool 15 minutes.

From: **Hintz's**
            North Star Lodge
              Starlake, Wisconsin

Fresh Vegetables
in Puff Pastry

cauliflower, broccoli flowerettes
puff pastry squares
cheese

Preheat oven to 400 degrees.

Cut puff pastry into 5″ squares. Place a thin slice of your favorite cheese on top of pastry.

Arrange flowerettes of your favorite vegetables on top of the cheese and pastry.

Carefully wrap the puff pastry around the

vegetables, cover with an egg wash and place on baking pan.

Bake approximately 20 minutes or until golden brown.

Note: The puff pastry may be made from scratch or purchased ready-made from most food stores.

From: **Timmer's on Big Cedar Lake**
5151 Timmer's Bay Drive
West Bend, Wisconsin

Wild Rice Dressing

1 pkg. wild & long grain rice mix
1 lb. pork sausage
1 rib celery
1 small onion
1 8-oz. can mushrooms
2 ozs. almonds, sliced

Cook rice according to package directions. Fry pork sausage until brown and crumbly. Drain off grease. Chop onion and celery fine. Drain mushrooms, toast almonds in frying pan in small amount of butter, stirring constantly. Drain. Mix all ingredients together. Put in casserole dish, bake at 350 degrees until heated through. Yield: 1½ quart casserole.

From: **Leffel's Supper Club**
1319 Forest Avenue
Antigo, Wisconsin

BRUNCH

Bread, Rolls, Muffins

Breads, Rolls, Muffins

One of the benefits of a more health conscious public has been the increased attention paid to bread. Often taken for granted and overlooked as a source of culinary variety, it is back in favor as cooks everywhere come up with wonderful new breads and revive interest in the old, time-tested recipes.

Nothing beats the smell of bread or muffins or biscuits baking in the oven. Make sure your butter dish is full before you put the bread in the oven, because there will be a line waiting for it when it comes out. Try some of these and see if you don't agree that bread baking is just about the best smell there is.

Bread, we are told, is the staff of life. Given life with leavening and human muscle, bread, home baked, returns life measure for measure.

Baking Powder Biscuit Mix

8 cups flour
6 Tbsps. baking powder
2 tsps. salt
½ cup non-fat dry milk
1 lb. margarine

Combine dry ingredients and mix well. Cut in margarine and continue to mix until mixture resembles coarse corn meal. Store in a tightly covered container.

To Make Biscuits from Mix:
3 cups Biscuit Mix
¾ cup lukewarm water

Mix well, Drop by spoonfuls on greased baking sheet and bake at 450 degrees for 7-10 minutes. Makes 18 biscuits.

Can be served with butter and jelly or topped with crushed berries in season.

From: **The Star Lake Saloon and Eatery**
Starlake, Wisconsin

Bran Muffins

3 cups buttermilk
3 cups bran
1 cup oil
3 eggs
1 cup brown sugar
1 cup white sugar
1 tsp. vanilla
3 tsps. baking soda
2 tsps. salt
1 cup raisins
3 cups flour
3 tsps. baking powder

Mix buttermilk and bran, let stand. Mix oil, eggs, brown and white sugar. Add vanilla, baking soda, salt and raisins. Mix three cups flour with 3 teaspoons baking powder. Mix the bran mixture with the liquids. Quickly blend in the flour mixture. Fill greased muffin tins two-thirds full. Bake for 25 minutes at 350 degrees.

These freeze beautifully. To reheat, wrap in foil and warm. Yield: 3 dozen muffins.

From: **The Duke House**
Mineral Point, Wisconsin

Infamous Fruit and Honey Bran Muffins

4 eggs
1 quart buttermilk
1 cup oil
½ jar applesauce
1 cup honey
5 cups flour
2 Tbsps. baking soda
2 tsps. salt
2 Tbsps. cinnamon
2 tsps. nutmeg
2 cups dried fruit mix
1 cup raisins
1 16-oz. box bran flakes
½ cup bran, if desired

Mix together wet ingredients. Combine wet and dry ingredients and mix well. Add bran flakes (and bran). Mix well. Refrigerate in closed container for 24 hours. Bake at 350 degrees for 20 minutes.

From: **The Mill Road Cafe**
Mill Road
Galesville, Wisconsin

Raspberry Muffins

2 eggs
2 cups buttermilk
¼ lb. butter, melted
2 cups fresh raspberries, washed
4½ cups flour
1¼ cups sugar
2 tsps. baking soda
½ tsp. salt
½ tsp. allspice

Have all ingredients at room temperature. Heat oven to 425 degrees. Grease muffin tins or line with paper cups. Sift flour, sugar, soda, salt and allspice together. Beat eggs and buttermilk. Add melted butter. Stir. Add half of dry ingredients and lightly mix. Add raspberries and lightly mix. Add remaining dry ingredients and mix lightly to moisten. Spoon into tins three-quarters full and top with a sprinkle of sugar. Bake 18-22 minutes. Yield: 2 dozen muffins.

From: **Quivey's Grove**
6261 Nesbit Road
Madison, Wisconsin

Pumpkin Muffins

2½ cups flour
3 cups brown sugar
2 tsps. baking soda
1 tsp. cinnamon
1 tsp. nutmeg
1 tsp. cloves
1½ cups pumpkin puree
4 beaten eggs
1 cup oil
⅔ cup water

Mix dry ingredients together. Mix wet ingredients together. Fold dry ingredients into wet ingredients, stirring until well mixed. Do not overmix. Fill greased muffin tins two-thirds full and bake in oven at 350 degrees for 30-40 minutes or until toothpick inserted in the center of a muffin comes out clean. Yield: 24 muffins.

From: **The Cafe Palms**
636 West Washington Avenue
Madison, Wisconsin

Highland Oat Scones

1½ cups flour
½ cup quick cooking oats
⅓ cup sugar
½ cup raisins
⅓ cup skim milk
⅓ cup melted butter
1 egg
1 Tbsp. baking powder
½ tsp. salt

Preheat oven to 375 degrees. Mix all ingredients well. Roll the mixture between two sheets of waxed paper. Cut into desired shapes, either circles or diamonds. Place on cookie sheet. Prepare the topping.

Topping:
1 Tbsp. sugar
1 Tbsp. melted butter
½ tsp. cinnamon

Brush the scones with topping mixture. Bake 14-16 minutes. Yield: 14-16 scones.

From: **The Duke House**
Mineral Point, Wisconsin

Blueberry Coffeecake

2 cups fresh or
  frozen blueberries
½ lb. butter
1½ cups sugar
5 eggs
2¼ cups sour cream
4 cups white flour
1 Tbsp. baking powder
2 tsps. baking soda
1½ tsps. vanilla extract

Cream the butter and sugar together. Add the eggs and sour cream, mixing well. Then add the flour, baking powder, baking soda and vanilla extract. Spread one-half mixture in 2 buttered 8"x12" pans. Place 1 cup fresh or frozen blueberries on top of each pan. Spread the other half of the mixture on top of the blueberries in both pans. Sprinkle topping mixture over all. Bake at 325 degrees for 1 hour or until done. Yields: 2 coffeecakes.

Topping:
2 cups brown sugar
3 Tbsps. cinnamon
1 cups chopped nuts
  of your choice

From: **The White Gull Inn**
Fish Creek, Wisconsin

Peaches and Cream Coffeecake

2 cups all-purpose flour
½ cup sugar
3 tsps. baking powder
½ tsp. salt
6 Tbsps. butter
1 cup milk
½ tsp. vanilla extract
1 egg, slightly beaten

3 oz. cream cheese
½ cup sour cream

1 small can sliced peaches,
 drained

Topping:
¼ cup sugar
2 Tbsps. butter
2 Tbsps. flour

Measure flour. In medium bowl, combine flour, sugar, baking powder and salt, blend well. Using fork, cut in butter until mixture is crumbly. Add milk, vanilla and egg, mixing well. Pour batter in greased and floured pan.

Mix cream cheese and sour cream until soft. Spread over batter and arrange peach slices over top.

In small bowl, combine all topping ingredients until crumbly, sprinkle over peaches.

Bake at 350 degrees for 25 to 45 minutes or until toothpick inserted in center comes out clean. Cool, cut into squares and serve warm. Yield: 1 coffeecake.

From: **The Ovens of Brittany
—East**
1718 Fordem Road
Madison, Wisconsin

Anise Bread

2 eggs
⅔ cup sugar
1½ tsps. anise seed
1 cup flour

Preheat the oven to 375 degrees. Grease and flour a loaf pan. Beat the eggs, gradually adding the sugar, anise and flour. Pour into the pan and bake 50-60 minutes.

From: **The Duke House**
Mineral Point, Wisconsin

Spicy Apple Cinnamon Bread

4 cups apples, finely chopped
6 eggs, lightly beaten
2 cups oil
4 cups sugar
4 tsps. vanilla extract
2 tsps. salt
2 tsps. cinnamon
6 cups flour
2 tsps. baking soda
1 tsp. baking powder

Chop apples first. Allow apples to drain thoroughly. Beat apples together with eggs, oil, sugar and vanilla.

Combine remaining ingredients and blend well. Bake in greased and floured bread tins at 325 degrees for approximately 1 hour or until toothpick inserted in middle of loaf comes out clean. Yield: 4 loaves.

From: **The Vintage House**
Hwy. 13 North
Wisconsin Rapids, Wisconsin

Orange Nut Loaf

1½ cups sugar
½ tsp. salt
1 egg
1½ cups flour
⅞ cup milk
3 ozs. fresh butter
¼ tsp. baking soda
2 oranges, ground up
1 Tbsp. baking powder
1 cup pitted, chopped dates

Mix all ingredients thoroughly and put in greased and floured bread tins. Bake at 375 degrees about 30 minutes until well browned. Insert toothpick in center to test for doneness. Yield: 3 loaves.

From: **The Round Barn**
Hwy. 14 East
Spring Green, Wisconsin

Apricot Puffs

8 oz. good apricot jam
1 tsp. cornstarch
dash of brandy

Heat the jam and brandy in saucepan over medium heat until warm. Sprinkle in cornstarch, stir over heat until thickened. Cool. Put into puff pastry squares.

Use your favorite recipe for puff pastry. (The Joy of Cooking has a reliable one.)

Roll the dough out on a well-floured surface until it is $1/16''$. Cut into 3" squares. Fill with apricot filling and fold over to make a triangle.

Bake at 350 degrees for 20 minutes or until golden brown. Dust with powdered sugar. Serve warm.

From: **The Fess Hotel**
123 Doty Street
Madison, Wisconsin

Walnut Whole Wheat Bread

1 cup water, 100-110 degrees
¼ cup brown sugar
1 Tbsp. dry yeast

1 egg, slightly beaten
3 Tbsp. walnut oil
1 tsp. salt

½ cup whole wheat flour
1½ cups chopped walnuts
3 cups white flour, approximately

Combine first three ingredients. Mix the next three ingredients together and add to the yeast mixture.

Add whole wheat flour and half of the white flour to the mixture. Beat well. Add walnuts, another cup of the flour and mix well. Add remaining flour, a little at a time (it may take more or less) until good consistency is reached. Knead well, let rise until doubled, 1 hour, punch down and let rise a second time, 30-45 minutes. Shape bread and let rise until doubled. Glaze with a mixture of beaten egg and 1 teaspoon salt. Bake at 375 degrees, 16-20 minutes until golden brown. Yield: 6 small loaves.

From: **Inn of the**
                          Four Seasons
                     Hwy. 99 and County E
                         Eagle, Wisconsin

Nut Roll

½ cup sugar
⅓ cup butter
2 cups scalded milk
1 tsp. vanilla extract
3 egg yolks
2 Tbsps. dry yeast
½ cup warm water
7-7½ cups flour

Filling:
3 egg whites
6 cups finely ground walnuts
1 tsp. vanilla extract
¼ cup melted butter
½ cup scalded milk
1 cup sugar
½ tsp. salt
1 tsp. cinnamon

Cream butter and sugar. Scald the milk and add to the butter and sugar, along with vanilla extract. Cool. Mix 3 egg yolks, yeast and water to milk mixture. Add 4 cups of flour and beat vigorously until smooth. Add about 2½-3 cups of remaining flour and knead the dough for 10 minutes. Place in a warm, well-greased bowl. Cover with a damp cloth and let rise 1½ hours.

Make the filling by beating the egg whites until stiff. Mix the remaining ingredients together well and fold in the egg whites. Roll the dough on a floured cloth. Spread the nut mixture on the dough being careful not to cover the dough too thickly. Roll up in a jelly roll fashion and bake in a jelly roll pan at 350 degrees for 1 hour. Dust with powdered sugar when cool.

From: **The Duke House**
Mineral Point, Wisconsin

BREADS, ROLLS, MUFFINS

Appetizers

Appetizers

Webster's New World Dictionary defines an appetizer as "n. a tasty food that stimulates the appetite." Everything that was submitted by Wisconsin restaurants certainly fits that description. See if you don't agree.

Cranberry Frost

1 cup chilled Wisconsin
  cranberry cocktail
½ cup raspberry sherbet

Place in blender, blend till smooth. Serve in juice glasses. Yield: 2 portions.

This is a popular appetizer especially during the summer months. A flavorful, simple recipe easily adapted to any number of portions.

From: **Sunrise Lodge**
          Land O' Lakes, Wisconsin

Morel Tart

3 Tbsps. unsalted butter
2 Tbsps. minced shallots
2 cups sliced, cleaned morels
4 small, prebaked tart shells,
  2½" each
1 oz. Cognac or Maderia
3 Tbsps. chicken glace
  (highly reduced chicken stock)

Saute the shallots in butter. Add sliced morels and saute until tender. Remove from the pan with slotted spoon. Reduce morel essence (liquid) over high heat, until it is nearly evaporated. Add Cognac and chicken glace. Reduce further until thick. Add morels and coat them with the thick glace. Fill tart shells. Sprinkle with minced parsley. Serve as a first course.

From: **Chez Michel**
          7601 Mineral Point Road
          Madison, Wisconsin

Seafood Sausage with Lemon Herb Sauce

Seafood Sausage:
½ lb. lemon sole fillets
½ lb. salmon steak, skinned
   boned & chopped coarsely
¼ lb. shrimp, deveined,
   shelled & chopped coarsely
¼ cup heavy cream
¼ tsp. salt
¼ tsp. white pepper
1 tsp. fresh parsley leaves,
   minced

Sauce:
¼ cup dry white wine
1 Tbsp. fresh lemon juice
1 tsp. white wine vinegar
½ cup butter, in pieces
½ tsp. freshly grated lemon rind
1 tsp. minced scallion
1 tsp. minced fresh parsley
Cayenne to taste

In a food processor or blender puree the sole, scraping down the sides of the bowl several times and chill the puree, covered for 30 minutes.

In another bowl, chill the shrimp and the salmon, covered, for 1 hour and 30 minutes.

In the food processor, blend the sole puree, eggs, cream, salt and pepper until the mixture is combined well. Transfer the mixture to a bowl and chill covered for 1 hour.

Fold the shrimp, salmon and parsley into the sole mixture. Divide the mixture between two 12″ square sheets of Saran Wrap and form into 2 logs, using the Saran Wrap to roll it. Twist the ends securely. Wrap each sausage securely in foil and poach the sausages in a kettle of simmering water for 10 to 15 minutes or until a metal skewer inserted in the center comes out hot. Transfer the sausage to a cutting board and let stand for 10 minutes.

In a small, heavy saucepan, boil the wine, lemon juice and vinegar until reduced by half. Reduce the heat to low and whisk in the butter bit by bit. Whisk in the lemon rind, scallion, parsley and dill. Add cayenne and salt to taste.

Pour sauce onto serving plates. Cut the sausage into ¾″ slices and lay on the sauce. Garnish with whole cooked shrimp, if desired.

From: **Carver's on the Lake**
799 Inlet Road
Green Lake, Wisconsin

Leek and Chevre Tarts

Pastry:
1 cup all-purpose flour
1 oz. goat cheese
such as Montrachet
¼ tsp. salt
2 ozs. cream cheese
(preferably w/o gum stabilizer)

For the crust, place all the ingredients in the bowl of a food processor and process until mixture forms a ball. The dough may also be made by simply mixing the ingredients with the fingers. Chill pastry if it appears too soft to handle. Divide the dough into 6 pieces and line six 4" tart shells. Chill pastry shells, line with foil and weight with rice or dry beans. Preheat oven to 475 degrees. Bake shells for 5 minutes, remove from oven and remove foil and weights. Reduce oven temperature to 375 degrees and return shells to oven to dry for 3-5 minutes.

Filling:
2-3 ozs. olive oil
6-8 ozs. soft, white
goat's cheese, again something
similar to a Montrachet
1 oz. extra virgin olive oil
5-6 cups sliced leeks
fresh herbs; thyme, savory, etc.

For the filling, gently saute leeks in olive oil until they are soft and reduced somewhat. Season to taste with salt and white pepper. Spread leeks into prebaked tart shells. Crumble goat's cheese over the leeks. Dribble the green olive oil over the tarts. Sprinkle with the fresh herbs. Bake in 375 degree oven until cheese is puffed and slightly browned. Serve. Yield: 6 servings.

From: **L'Etoile**
25 N. Pinckney
Madison, Wisconsin

Clams Renaissance

25 fresh clams (retain shells)
⅛ cup diced green peppers
¼ cup finely diced onion
2 garlic cloves
¼ cup dry bread crumbs
¼ tsp. basil
½ Tbsp. Lawry's seasoning salt
1 tsp. Worcestershire sauce
2 tsps. fresh, chopped parsley
4 strips bacon
white wine

Cook clams (poach). Drain and save liquid. Chop clams. Saute peppers, onions, garlic in 2 tablespoons of butter. Add clams. Pick up butter with 2 tablespoons of flour. Add liquid from clams.

Combine all ingredients except bacon and wine. Fill 24 shells with mixture. Top each shell with a small piece of bacon. Heat in a 375 degree oven for 10 minutes.

Remove and finish with a dash of white wine. Garnish with lemon and parsley sprig. Yield: 12 servings of 2 each.

From:
**Faller's
Seafood Restaurant at
The Renaissance Inn**
414 Maple Drive
Sister Bay, Wisconsin

Quenelles of Scallops
with Lobster,
Gewurtztraminer Beurre Blanc,
Wild Mushrooms and Grilled Radicchio

Quenelles:
4 ozs. sea scallops
salt, white pepper,
  nutmeg to taste
½ egg white
½ cup heavy cream

For quenelles, place scallops, salt, pepper, and nutmeg in food processor. Turn on for about 30 seconds. Scrape down mixture and add egg white and process 1 minute. Let rest in refrigerator for 15 minutes and add cream

in processor in steady stream. With spoon, form quenelles into ovals about the size of a small egg. Poach about 5 minutes in a mixture of one-half white wine and one-half fish stock, covered by a buttered paper.

Grilled Radicchio:

2 small heads radicchio
salt & pepper to taste
Extra Virgin olive oil

Cut radicchio into quarters attached by the core. Blanch for 30 seconds in boiling salted water. Cool and drain. Form into shape similar to the quenelles. Coat with olive oil, salt and pepper. Grill or char-broil till hot. About 3 minutes per side.

Gewurtztraminer Beurre Blanc:

3 shallots, chopped
½ bottle Gewurtztraminer
salt & white pepper to taste
½ quart heavy cream
6 ozs. butter

Saute shallots for Gewurtztraminer Beurre Blanc in 1 tsp. butter for 10 seconds. Add wine and reduce by two-thirds. Add cream and reduce by two-thirds. Then whip in remaining soft butter. Remove from direct heat and keep warm.

Lobster and Wild Mushrooms:

4 ozs. julienne lobster
4 ozs. julienne of wild mushrooms
  (shitakes, morels,
  or chanterelles)
1 tsp. butter
1 tsp. shallots, chopped
salt & pinch cayenne pepper

Saute lobster, mushrooms and shallots in butter. Add seasonings.

Set up plate with 2 quenelles, 2 pieces of radicchio, lobster and mushroom salad in the center and 2-3 oz. sauce around. Serves 4.

From: **John Byron's**
777 E. Michigan Avenue
Galleria Level
Milwaukee, Wisconsin

Seafood Triangles
with Spicy Red Curry Sauce

1 Tbsp. butter
1 Tbsp. flour
½ cup milk
salt to taste

1 Tbsp. butter
4 green spring onions
1 sm. pkg. frozen,
  chopped spinach
¾ cup cooked, flaked crabmeat
¾ cup cooked shrimp, small
1 Tbsp. lemon juice
pinch of nutmeg
freshly ground pepper
¼ tsp. granulated garlic

Melt butter in small saucepan, add flour, stirring over low heat for about 1 minute or until light golden in color. Add milk, stir until thoroughly blended. Set aside.

Heat butter in small saute pan, add onions and spinach, cook for about 3 minutes, lower heat, stir in prepared sauce, crabmeat, shrimp, lemon juice, nutmeg and pepper and garlic. Allow to cool.

To make the triangles, take a package of phyllo sheets and lay the sheets out flat on a work surface, cover with a slightly dampened towel (this prevents pastry from drying out). Cut pastry into strips 8″ wide—take one strip at a time, brush with melted butter, fold strip to form a 4″ strip, brush the top with melted butter. Place 1 tablespoon cooled filling on the bottom corner of the strip, fold pastry over the filling to form a triangle, continue folding—keeping the triangle shape as you go. Brush the triangle with butter. Place triangles, seam side down on baking pan—allow room for the triangles to expand and puff. Bake in a 425 degree oven until puffed and golden or about 15 minutes. Serve with Spicy Red Curry Sauce on the side. Yield: 8 servings.

Spicy Red Curry Sauce

1 oz. butter
1 Tbsp. flour
⅓ cup cream
⅔ cup chicken broth
1 Tbsp. tomato sauce

Melt butter in heavy based saucepan, add flour and cook, stirring for 1-2 minutes. Remove pan from heat and gradually stir in cream and chicken broth, add tomato sauce, curry paste (or curry powder) and white pepper.

1 Tbsp. Pataks Madras
   Curry Paste*
white pepper to taste

Return pan to heat and bring slowly to a boil, stirring constantly. Reduce heat and simmer about 8 minutes. Serve on the side with Seafood Triangles.
   *Curry powder may be substituted.

From: **Faller's
Seafood Restaurant at
The Renaissance Inn**
414 Maple Drive
Sister Bay, Wisconsin

Borek with Cheese Filling

½ lb. feta cheese
¼ lb. cream cheese
⅛ tsp. nutmeg
2 eggs
1 1-lb. pkg. phyllo dough
½ lb. unsalted butter, melted,
   (may need more)

Cream cheeses together, using a mixer, food processor, or by hand. Add the nutmeg. Add the eggs, one at a time. Continue mixing until smooth. Butter one strip of phyllo dough (using a pastry brush). Place one teaspoon of filling on lower left-hand corner of dough. Fold the other corner over to make a triangle. Fold the remainder of the dough as you would a flag (up and over). Lay finished triangle on baking sheet, and brush the top with butter. Continue with the rest of the dough. Borek may be covered and frozen at this point. Bake for 15-20 minutes at 350 degrees. Serve immediately.

Leftover borek may be frozen and reheated. The filling may be prepared a few days in advance.

From: **The Jamieson House**
Poynette, Wisconsin

Smoked Trout Puffs

Puffs:
½ cup water
½ cup milk
¼ lb. butter
1 tsp. salt
1½ tsps. sugar
1 cup flour
5 eggs, room temperature

For puff pastry, heat water, milk, butter, salt and sugar to a boil. Add flour all at once and with wooden spoon over medium heat, beat and cook until it forms a large, stiff ball and is difficult to work. Remove from heat and beat in eggs *one* at a time, keeping paste stiff. Grease and flour a baking sheet. Fill pastry bag with one-half open tip, with the paste and pipe out little puffs, about 1" in diameter and 1" high. Bake at 425 degrees without disturbing 10 minutes. Lower heat to 350 degrees and bake 10 minutes or until dry, puffed and set.

Smoked Trout Salad:
1 lb. cleaned, smoked trout,
    no bones, no skin
5 oz. onion, finely diced
1 tsp. Lawry seasoning salt
2 tsps. Dijon mustard
1 Tbsp. cream
5 ozs. celery, finely diced
1 Tbsp. lemon pepper seasoning
1 tsp. parsley flakes
2 tsps. ketchup
⅔ cup mayonnaise

For the salad, mix all the ingredients together. Split the puffs and fill with the salad.

From: **Quivey's Grove**
6261 Nesbit Road
Madison, Wisconsin

Soups

Soups

Making good soup is almost a necessity for surviving Wisconsin's winters. There is something about a bowl of hot, made-from-scratch soup, whether you made it yourself, someone made it for you, or you're eating in a restaurant, that makes you feel cared for, warm all through.

Wisconsin's chefs have recipes for old favorites with a new twist, some new soups and some traditions. Try them all and see if you don't agree: Wisconsin knows good soup.

Cream of Almond Soup

3 Tbsps. almond paste
1¼ cups chopped,
   toasted almonds
2 qts. chicken broth
3 egg yolks, slightly beaten
½ tsp. sugar
½ tsp. salt
2¼ cups heavy cream
¼ tsp. almond extract

Cook almond paste, almonds and broth together. Beat egg yolks with sugar and salt, adding to cooked broth. Add cream and almond extract and do not overheat!

This soup can be served hot or cold. Garnish with sliced almonds.

From: **The American Club**
          407 Highland Drive
          Kohler, Wisconsin

Cream of Asparagus Soup

1½ cups chopped, fresh
   asparagus w/o tips
   (save tips for garnish)
2 cups chicken stock
4 Tbsps. unsalted butter
¼ cup chopped onions
5½ Tbsps. flour
dry white wine
1 cup heavy cream
salt, white pepper &
   nutmeg to taste

Boil the chopped asparagus in the chicken stock until tender. Melt butter and saute the onions until translucent. Strain asparagus and reserve stock. Add the asparagus to the butter and onions, cook, stirring often. Add flour, a little bit at a time, and cook a few minutes. To this mixture add stock, white wine to taste, and cream. Season with salt, pepper, and nutmeg. Allow to cool for fifteen (15) minutes, stirring often. Process until smooth. An hour before serving add the asparagus tips. Yield: 5 cups.

From: **Chip and Py's**
          815 South 5th Street
          Milwaukee, Wisconsin

Cream of Broccoli and Mushroom Soup

½ stick margarine
1 cup finely diced, sweet onion
2 cups stems & pieces
canned mushrooms
3 qts. water
2 Tbsps. beef base
1 large head broccoli,
　cut in small pieces,
　peel & dice stems, too
cornstarch for thickening
1 pt. half & half

(When using beef base, do not add salt). Melt margarine in 6-quart soup pot. Add onions, and saute until soft. Do not brown. Add mushrooms, canning juice, water and beef base. When it comes to a good, rolling boil, add broccoli and diced stems. Cook only until tender crisp. Make a thickening of cornstarch and water. Stir into soup to a cream soup consistency. When thickened, take off heat and stir in half & half. Taste and correct seasoning.

From:　**Florena Supper Club**
N3380 Hwy. 13
Medford, Wisconsin

Cream of Cauliflower Soup

1 Tbsp. butter
¼ cup chopped onions
¼ cup sliced carrots
1 stalk celery, sliced
2 cups water
1 head cauliflower,
　broken into flowerets

In a large kettle, heat butter and saute onions until tender, add carrots and celery and cook two minutes, then add water, bring to a boil. Now add all remaining ingredients, return to boil and simmer 5 minutes. Remove from heat, add prepared white sauce to kettle. Refrigerate overnight. Yield: 6 cups.

¼ *cup chicken soup base*
¼ *tsp. pepper*
1 *tsp. parsley*
¼ *tsp. bouquet garni*
1 *bay leaf*
¼ *tsp. curry powder*
3 *cups white sauce*

From: **The Kitchen Table**
East Third and Maple Streets
Marshfield, Wisconsin

Creme of Leek and Shrimp Soup

1½ *lbs. shrimp, in the shell,*
   26-30 count
1½ *qts. chicken stock*
2 *Tbsps. butter*
4 *ozs. Prosciutto or ham fat, diced*
6 *medium leeks*
½ *lb. shallots*
½ *lb. carrots*
1 *bay leaf*
5 *peppercorns, crushed*
10 *sprigs fresh thyme*
1 *bunch parsley stems*
2 *cups white wine*
½ *qt. heavy cream,*
   reduced to 1 pt.

Bring shrimp to a boil in chicken stock. Cover, turn off heat and let sit for 3 minutes. Remove shrimp and reserve stock. When shrimp are cool, peel and devein (save shells). Saute ham fat in butter. Add shrimp shells, 5 leeks (sliced and cleaned), shallots, carrots, bay leaf, peppercorns, thyme and parsley stems. Saute until vegetables are tender. Add white wine and reduce by one-half. Add chicken stock and simmer for 45 minutes to 1 hour. Put in food processor and puree until fine. Strain through a medium china cap. Bring back to a boil and add heavy cream, and garnish with shrimp which have been cut in half on the bias, and blanched julienne of two-thirds (white and light green part) of the last leek. Salt and pepper to taste.

From: **John Byron's**
777 E. Michigan Avenue,
Galleria Level
Milwaukee, Wisconsin

Chicken Almond Soup

1 cup chopped celery
2 cups chopped mushrooms
1 cup chopped onion

1 qt. chicken stock
white pepper to taste
2 cups cooked, boned chicken
2 Tbsps. almond extract

chicken fat or butter roux
cream or milk

Saute celery, onions and mushrooms in butter. Add the chicken stock, boned, cooked chicken, white pepper and almond extract.

Thicken with roux. Add cream or milk to bring to desired consistency. Garnish with slivered almonds on top.

From: **The White Gull Inn**
Fish Creek, Wisconsin

Cream of Mushroom Soup

1 Tbsp. butter
1 small clove garlic, crushed
2 Tbsps. onion, minced
1 lb. fresh mushrooms, sliced
4 cups chicken stock,
  from scratch

pinch nutmeg
salt to taste
dash Worcestershire sauce
dash accent
¼ tsp. ground black pepper
¼ cup dry white wine
dash tobasco

6 Tbsps. melted butter
flour for roux

1 cup half & half
chopped parsley
croutons

Melt butter in 2-quart soup pot. Saute garlic and onion until tender. Add mushrooms and saute until tender.

Add stock and bring to a boil. Simmer for twenty minutes. Add spices etc. to boiling soup. Adjust salt and pepper as necessary.

Heat melted butter. Add enough flour to make a roux. Cook the roux. Add the roux a little at a time to the boiling soup, while stirring, until a creamy consistency is reached. Stir until roux is completely dissolved.

Remove soup from heat and stir in half and half. Garnish with croutons and parsley.

From: **Karl Ratzsch's**
320 East Mason Street
Milwaukee, Wisconsin

Potato Cucumber Soup

1 lg. onion, chopped
1 Tbsp. butter
1 qt. water
2½ lbs. potatoes,
   peeled, sliced thinly
1 Tbsp. dill
½ cup chicken soup base
3 lg. cucumbers,
   peeled, seeded & cubed
2 tsps. white pepper
1½ cups sour cream

Saute onions in butter. Add water and bring to a boil. Add everything else and cook until potatoes are tender, about 10 minutes. Refrigerate soup overnight. Before reheating, stir in sour cream. Soup may also be served cold. Yield: 2½ quarts.

From: **The Kitchen Table**
East Third & Maple Streets
Marshfield, Wisconsin

Potato Cheese Soup

2 qts. potatoes, finely diced
1 cup onions, finely chopped
2 heaping Tbsps. chicken base
   (good quality)
½ lb. grated Cheddar cheese
1 qt. milk
2 Tbsps. chopped chives
½ lb. bacon, fried crisp & drained

Put potatoes, onions and soup base in a large kettle and cover with water. Cook until potatoes are tender. Add cheese and stir until it is melted. Add milk and chives. Heat but do not boil. Yield: 8 servings.

From: **Laffel's Supper Club**
1319 Forest Avenue
Antigo, Wisconsin

Sausage, Cheese and Beer Soup

2 qts. water
½ tsp. black pepper
smoked ham skin, bone or scraps
1 small onion, chopped
½ cup margarine
½ cup flour
2 cups cold milk
¾ lb. sharp Cheddar cheese
½ bottle beer
¾ lb. cooked breakfast
   sausage links

In a large pot, simmer water, black pepper, ham scraps, and onion for 1 hour. Strain, skim fat from surface and return to pot. Keep hot. Reserve ham scraps for another stock.

In another pot, prepare a roux. Melt margarine until bubbly and whisk in flour, cooking and stirring over medium heat for five minutes. Add hot broth, 2 cups at a time, whisking and cooking until thick and smooth after each addition.

Slowly add cold milk, stirring all the time. Soup should be fairly thick and very smooth.

Add grated cheese a little at a time, stirring until thick, smooth and melted. Open the beer. Drink half the bottle, add the rest to the soup (about ¾ cup). Chop the sausages into ½" lengths and add to the soup. Keep on low heat until ready to serve. Yield: 6-8 servings.

From:

Quivey's Grove
6261 Nesbit Road
Madison, Wisconsin

Cream of Vegetable Soup

4½ Tbsps. butter
½ cup flour
1⅓ cups milk
1 cup half & half or heavy cream
3 Tbsps. butter
1 cup chopped onion
⅔ cup chopped celery
⅔ cup chopped carrot
⅔ cup sliced mushrooms
⅔ cup chopped broccoli
1 clove garlic, minced
1 Tbsp. basil
1 Tbsp. thyme
3½ cups chicken stock
¼ cup dry white wine
salt
white pepper

To make the roux, melt the 4½ tablespoons of butter in a small, heavy saucepan. With a wooden spoon, stir in flour until well blended. Cook over low heat, stirring often, for 3-5 minutes. Remove from heat and set aside.

Chop onion, celery, carrot, broccoli. Slice mushrooms, mince garlic.

Heat milk and half & half (or heavy cream) together over low heat.

In a 3-quart saucepan or soup pot, melt 3 tablespoons of butter. Saute onion, celery, and carrot a few minutes. Add mushrooms, broccoli, basil and thyme, and continue to cook over medium heat until vegetables are almost tender. Stir in minced garlic and cook for 1-2 minutes more.

Add stock, bring to a boil, reduce to simmer.

Whisk in roux, continue to cook over medium heat until smooth, stirring often. Add hot milk mixture in 2 or 3 installments, whisking well after each addition. Add wine, simmer 10-15 minutes. Season to taste with salt and white pepper. Yield: 2 quarts, 6-8 servings.

The vegetables in this soup may vary with the seasons!

From: **The Ovens of Brittany
—East**
1718 Fordem Road
Madison, Wisconsin

Dill Pickle Soup

7 cups water
½ lb. soup bones
8 ozs. mixed vegetables
4 Tbsps. flour
½ to 1 cup sour cream
1 cup shredded dill pickles
1 cup dill pickle juice
salt

Rinse vegetables and soup bone, clean, prepare stock and drain off. Shred dill pickles into fine strips. Garnish soup with flour and cream, bring to a boil; add uncooked dill pickles and pickle juice, salt to taste. Heat. Serve with potato or dropped noodles.

From: **Cracovia Restaurant**
1531 West Lincoln Avenue
Milwaukee, Wisconsin

Southern Black Bean Soup

1 lb. black beans
2½ qts. ham stock
8 ozs. tomato paste
1 bay leaf
⅛ tsp. ground cloves
¼ tsp. pepper
¼ tsp. ground thyme
¼ tsp. dry mustard
2 ribs celery, diced
1 medium onion, diced
1 bacon rind
1 ham bone
1 Tbsp. melted butter
2 Tbsps. flour

Soak beans overnight. Add beans to stock and bring to a boil. Add tomato paste and seasonings. Add celery, onions, bacon rind and ham bone. Simmer 2 hours. Make a roux from the butter and flour, being careful not to brown it. Add the roux to the soup. Remove the rind and the ham bone. Garnish each bowl of soup with thin slices of lemon. Yield: about 2 quarts, 6-8 servings.

From: **Barth's at the Bridge**
N58 W6194 Columbia Road
Cedarburg, Wisconsin

Liver Dumpling Soup

1½ qts. chicken stock
⅓ cup chopped celery
⅓ cup chopped onion
dumpling batter
⅓ cup chopped tomato
1 Tbsp. chopped parsley

Put the chicken stock, celery, and onion in a soup kettle. Bring to a boil.

Roll the dumpling batter into 1" balls and drop in the soup.

Add the tomatoes and parsley and cook until the dumplings are plump and float to the top of the soup, about 10 or 15 minutes. Stir occasionally so that the dumplings don't stick to the bottom of the pan.

Dumpling Batter:
2 slices stale, white bread
¼ cup milk
¼ lb. chicken livers
1 Tbsp. unsalted butter
¼ cup finely chopped onion
2 egg whites
freshly ground black pepper
1 tsp. finely chopped parsley
½-1 cup dry bread crumbs

Soak the bread slices in the milk for about 5 minutes, then squeeze them dry. Run the bread and chicken livers through a meat grinder into a mixing bowl, or chop them together finely with a sharp knife.

Melt the butter in a heavy 10- or 12-inch skillet. When the foam subsides, add the onions. Cook them for about 8 minutes, or until they are lightly colored, then add them to the bread and liver mixture. Stir in the egg whites, salt, a few grindings of black pepper and the parsley. Add ½ cup bread crumbs, mix, then form 1 tablespoon of the mixture into a little ball. If it is too soft to hold together firmly, add more bread crumbs by the tablespoon. Dust your hands lightly with flour and form all the mixture into balls about 1" in diameter. Bring the soup to a boil and drop in the dumplings.

From: **Jack Pandl's**
Whitefish Bay Inn
1319 East Henry Clay Road
Whitefish Bay, Wisconsin

Tomato Dill Soup

4½ Tbsps. butter
½ cup flour
3 Tbsps. butter
1 cup diced onion
1 lg. clove garlic, minced
3¼ cups chicken stock
3 dashes tabasco
22-oz. can tomato puree
11-oz. can tomatoes, diced
2½ Tbsps. honey
¾ tsp. black pepper
¼ tsp. cayenne
½ tsp. chili powder
1 tsp. basil
1 Tbsp. dill weed

To make roux, melt 4½ tablespoons butter in small, heavy saucepan. Stir in flour until well blended. Cook over low heat, stirring often, for 3-5 minutes. Remove from heat and set aside.

Melt 3 tablespoons butter in 3-quart saucepan or soup pot. Saute diced onions until tender, then add minced garlic and saute 1-2 minutes more.

Add chicken stock, bring to a boil, reduce to a simmer.

Whisk in roux, whisk and cook over medium heat until somewhat thickened and smooth.

Add tabasco, honey, tomato products, and spices, stirring thoroughly after each addition. Simmer soup 30-45 minutes. Season further, if necessary, with salt and pepper.

From: **The Ovens of Brittany
—Monroe Street**
1831 Monroe Street
Madison, Wisconsin

Veal Ragout Soup

1 lb. veal, ¼" cubes
1 Tbsp. shortening
2 Tbsps. paprika
2 cups beef stock
2 cups chicken stock
1 carrot, diced
1 medium onion, diced
1 potato, ¼" cubes
1 bay leaf
½ cup rice
*½ cup sour cream

Put shortening in a frying pan, saute veal cubes until evenly browned on all sides. Add 2 tablespoons of paprika, stirring occasionally so that veal will not burn. Cook for approximately 5 to 10 minutes.

In a kettle add beef and chicken stock together. Add all the vegetables and the bay leaf, bring to a boil, back off to a simmer and simmer for 5 minutes. Then add meat to the kettle and simmer another 5 minutes.

Cook the rice until done, drain and wash, add to the soup. Yield: 8-10 servings.

*Note—the sour cream is optional. Add ½ teaspoon to each cup of soup just before serving.

From: **The Golden Mast Inn**
1270 Lacy's Lane
Okauchee, Wisconsin

Meat & Poultry

Meat & Poultry

Meat and poultry remain a staple of the American diet, whatever the current fad or phase seems to be. Chicken has become a mainstay because of modern production techniques. It used to be a luxury for all but the farmers who raised them and the wealthy who could afford chicken. In 1941 chicken cost 78 cents a pound and was much more expensive than beef, lamb or pork. Now, of course, chicken is one of the most affordable meats.

With the interest in cuisines different than our own, Americans have added duckling, goose, veal, and lamb to a diet that used to consist mostly of pork, beef and occasionally chicken and once or twice a year, turkey.

Wisconsin veal is known by restaurateurs all over the United States as the best available. I was once served a superb meal in a Philadelphia restaurant, cooked by the owner herself when she discovered that I was from Wisconsin. I felt a little like royalty, but she could not say enough about the wonders of Wisconsin veal.

Some of the best lamb I have ever eaten, I have eaten here. There is no comparison between farm lamb and range lamb when it comes to tenderness and flavor. Wisconsin farm lamb holds its own with the best.

The same can be said for duckling and goose, two birds that have become more popular and are now available fresh at farmers' markets and through butcher shops.

Here are new and interesting ways to cook some of Wisconsin's best.

Stuffed Chicken Breasts

4 10- to 12-oz. chicken breasts
¼ tsp. Hungarian paprika
½ cup sherry
¼ cup melted butter
white pepper to taste
salt to taste
half & half cream

Place breasts in roasting pan with other ingredients. Cover and bake at 350 degrees for 30 to 40 minutes. Remove breasts, strain juices. Bring juices to a boil, and thicken with a butter roux until desired consistency is reached. Remove from heat. Add hot half & half cream, again to desired consistency. Serve this sauce over chicken breasts.

Stuffing:
2 Tbsps. butter
⅛ cup chopped mushrooms
⅛ cup diced pimentos
⅛ cup chopped bacon
⅛ cup chopped celery
⅛ cup chopped green pepper
⅛ cup minced onion
1 bay leaf
1 cup cooked spinach, cooled
4 cups cooked white rice
3 ozs. anisette
dash nutmeg
¼ tsp. powdered garlic
dash Worcestershire sauce
½ tsp. salt
½ tsp. ground black pepper

Melt butter in saute pan. Saute mushrooms, pimentos, bacon, celery, green pepper, onion and bay leaf until tender. Cool. Combine this mixture with spinach, rice, anisette, and remaining ingredients. Stuff each breast with about ½ cup of stuffing.

From: **Karl Ratzsch's**
320 East Mason Street
Milwaukee, Wisconsin

Pappas' Stuffed Chicken Breast

8 skinned and boned chicken
  breasts, 6-8 ozs. each
2 ozs. Monterey Jack cheese,
  shredded
2 ozs. Cheddar cheese, shredded
2 ozs. Swiss cheese, shredded
1 oz. Parmesan cheese,
  grated fine
12 strips of bacon,
  4 cooked crisp & crumbled
2 lg. eggs, slightly beaten
  before adding to cheese mixture
⅛ tsp. white pepper, ground
pinch of salt

Take the Monterey Jack, Cheddar, Swiss cheese and the grated Parmesan, along with the crumbled bacon and put in a bowl. Add slightly beaten eggs as the binding agent. Season mixture with salt and pepper. Use an ice cream scoop or roll into eight equal size balls with your hands. Fill each chicken breast with the cheese, bacon, and egg mixture. Wrap one strip of bacon around each stuffed chicken breast, using a toothpick to hold the bacon on. Bake on a greased pan for 1 hour at a temperature of 350 degrees. If the bacon around the chicken doesn't get done as much as you would like, turn oven to a higher temperature for a few extra minutes. Keep checking so the bacon doesn't start to burn. Delicious with rice pilaf or potatoes of your choice. Yield: 8 servings.

From: **Michael's Restaurant**
1815 Ward Avenue
LaCrosse, Wisconsin

Deviled Chicken

8 10-oz. boneless breasts
¾ cup Chablis wine
paprika
¾ cup Dijon mustard
bread crumbs

Combine mustard and chablis, mix well.
  Brush breasts lightly with oil and place on grill in broiler, skin side down. Brush with mustard sauce. Let one side cook for 2-3 minutes. Turn breast, and brush other side

with sauce. Breasts will be done when side flaps start to curl. Brush skin side with more sauce, top lightly with bread crumbs, sprinkle with paprika and place back under broiler until browned.

From: **The Red Geranium**
Hwy. 50E
Lake Geneva, Wisconsin

Chicken Richelieu

Stuffing:
½ cup minced ham
½ cup minced walnuts
1 oz. brandy
½ cup minced onion
½ cup minced mushrooms
⅛ cup butter

Saute all ingredients until they form a paste—about 10 minutes.

Remove the skin from 4 chicken breasts, 6-8 ounces each, and pound out until ⅛" thick. Put ½ cup filling in the middle of each and roll up. Roll in a little flour, then in beaten egg, then in bread crumbs. Bake for about 10-15 minutes at 375 degrees, turning once. Serve with sauce.

Sauce:
2 pts. half & half
2 Tbsps. dill weed
¼ cup chicken stock
1 Tbsp. Grey Poupon mustard
2 cups Asiago cheese

Heat ingredients together. Thicken with roux from ¼ cup butter and ½ cup flour. Then add cheese and heat through.

From: **The Ovens of Brittany
—Monroe Street**
1831 Monroe Street
Madison, Wisconsin

Croustade of Duckling
with Red Cabbage and Cracklings, Black Truffle Sauce

2 cloves garlic, chopped
4 shallots, diced
2 cups white wine
½ cup brandy
Meat from ½ boned duck, diced
½ lb. pork butt, diced
⅛ tsp. ground thyme
½ pinch each, ground cloves,
cinnamon, nutmeg, coriander
¼ cup pistachios, shelled
1 egg
½ bunch parsley stems, chopped

Saute garlic and shallots for 30 seconds. Add wine and brandy and reduce to ¼ cup. Cool. Put duck meat and pork in food processor with spices and herbs. Grind about 20 seconds. Add egg and wine/brandy reduction and process 10 more seconds. Cook small patty to test for seasonings. Roll into sausage size with silicon paper or aluminum foil and bake in 400 degree oven until juices run clear.

Puff Pastry:
1 lb. butter
1 cup water
1 lb. flour
1 tsp. salt

Mix ice water, 14 oz. bread flour, salt and 2 ounces butter into a dough, medium stiff. Remove from mixer, round into a ball and allow to stand in refrigerator for 15 minutes. Mix 14 ounces butter with 2 ounces cake or bread flour in the mixer until holding together. Form the butter into squares. Roll the dough following the direction of the four corners, leaving the center thicker. Place the butter in the center and lap over the four sides, flatten with the roling pin by gently pounding the dough. Roll out again ½" thick and twice as long as wide. Brush off excess flour. Fold both ends towards the middle and then double again. Let rest 15 minutes, repeating the rolling process and give 2 of these turns and 2 rolls resulting in a 3-way fold.

Puff Pastry Box:
Roll out dough in 4 rectangles, 2"x4"x¼" thick. Egg wash the top and cut inside of the rectangle about ¼" around the inside and ⅛" deep. Bake at 400 degrees for 5 minutes, then 375 degrees for 8 minutes. Remove top and scrape out inside dough.

Red Cabbage with Cracklings

Rendered duck skin, cubed
2 ozs. rendered duck fat
½ head red cabbage, sliced thin
Salt and pepper to taste
1 oz. balsamic vinegar

Render down duck skin from duck sausage until brown and crisp. Drain fat and reserve. Dice duck cracklings. Place duck fat in saute pan and saute cabbage with salt and pepper about 10 seconds. Add vinegar and cook 5 more seconds.

Black Truffle Sauce

1 qt. duck stock
1 oz. julienned black truffle and juice
3 ozs. balsamic vinegar

Reduce the vinegar and truffle and juice by one-half. Add duck stock and reduce to 1½ cups.

Duck Stock:
In oven, brown off back bones from duck sausage with 1 onion, diced and 1 small carrot. When brown, add 1 rib of celery, 1 bay leaf, 4 cloves garlic, ½ tsp. thyme, parsley stems and 6 peppercorns. Add 1 quart white wine and 1 quart chicken stock and simmer slowly for 2 hours. Strain off the stock.

Set-Up:
Slice duck sausage and place on top of puff pastry box. Place cabbage around the box and pour sauce over the sausage and around the plate. Garnish cabbage with cracklings.

From: **John Byron's**
777 E. Michigan Avenue
Galleria Level
Milwaukee, Wisconsin

Salmi of Duck a la Ratzsch

4 10-oz. duck breasts
2 tsps. Lawry's seasoned salt
1 tsp. black pepper
1 lg. onion, chopped
3 cups duck, chicken stock
3 ozs. olive juice
  (from stuffed green olives)
¾ cup cherry juice
  (from tart, pitted cherries)

2 cups tart, pitted cherries
½ cup sliced, stuffed green olives
2 Tbsps. sugar
¼ cup melted butter
flour
Kitchen Bouquet
2 ozs. burgundy

Place duck breasts in roasting pan, season with salt and pepper, add chopped onion. Bake at 425 degrees until skin starts to brown.

Reduce oven temperature to 350 degrees. Add stock, juices, and wine to breasts. Bake for 45 minutes or until tender. Skin should be golden brown and crisp.

Remove breasts from pan and keep warm. Strain pan juices into saucepan. Bring to a boil. Add cherries, olives, sugar and burgundy. Return to a brisk boil. Make a roux with butter and flour and add to stock until desired consistency is reached. Add enough Kitchen Bouquet to get rich, brown color. Serve breasts on a bed of wild rice. Cover the breasts with sauce.

From: **Karl Ratzsch's**
320 East Mason Street
Milwaukee, Wisconsin

Duck Chasseur

1 duckling
salt and pepper
garlic to taste
3 ozs. clarified butter
3 ozs. sherry
4 ozs. standard brown sauce
½ cup chopped tomatoes
½ cup chopped green onion
½ cup chopped fresh mushrooms
chopped parsley to garnish

Season the duck with salt, pepper and garlic. Roast at 350 degrees until tender, approximately 3½ hours or until cavity juices run clear.

Cut the duck into quarters, removing wing tips, dredge in flour. Saute in 3 ounces clarified butter. When brown, turn, reduce heat. Add 3 ounces sherry and let reduce. Add 4 ounces standard brown sauce, tomatoes, mushrooms, and onions.

Simmer for 15 minutes. Place duck on heated platter, add 2 tablespoons butter to sauce and reduce to desired consistency.

Pour sauce over duck and garnish with finely chopped parsley.

Serve with wild rice and appropriate vegetable.

From: **The Vintage House**
Hwy. 13 North
Wisconsin Rapids, Wisconsin

Duck a l'Orange

Duck a l'Orange is served at Bernard's with a wild rice and brown rice risotto and stewed spiced sweet potato piped on top of a pineapple slice.

2 whole 4-5 lb. young
　Wisconsin ducklings
¼ tsp. leaf oregano
1 medium onion
1 medium carrot
2 stalks of celery
1 medium parsnip
1 qt. water
4 Tbsps. vegetable shortening
5 Tbsps. flour
4 ozs. orange juice concentrate
1 orange
¼ tsp. salt
1 pinch ground cloves
1 pinch ground cardamom
1 pinch ground ginger
2 ozs. Grand Marnier
1 oz. Cognac
2 Tbsps. Kitchen Bouquet

One Day Ahead:

Preheat oven to 375 degrees. Check temperature with oven thermometer as correct oven temperature is very important. Cut neck and wings off ducklings and put aside. Take paper towel and thoroughly dry cavity and outside of duckling. Rub skin and cavity with salt. Sprinkle leaf oregano into cavity. Grease roasting pan well with shortening. Place ducklings, breast up, in roasting pan. Do not cover. Place in center of oven. Roast for approximately 1 hour and 45 minutes, or until golden brown, occasionally moving ducklings in pan to prevent from sticking. This will not completely finish cooking the ducklings. Remove from oven. Place ducklings immediately on a rack or paper towel to drain any excess fat. Take neck, wings, gizzard of ducklings and chop with cleaver into 1" pieces. Cut vegetables into 1" pieces. Put in same pan duck was roasted in. When ducklings are cooled, carve off breasts and legs, wrap tightly and refrigerate. Now chop bones of ducklings into small pieces and add to roaster. Place in oven at 400 degrees for 30 minutes occasionally stirring vegetables and duck parts until they turn lightly brown. Now pour 1 quart of water over mixture and let cook for a few minutes on top of stove over high heat, stirring well. Make sure all the baked on brown crust in the roaster gets dissolved. If you have a 6-quart pressure cooker available, pour the mixture into that and let simmer for at least 2 hours. If you don't have a pressure cooker, use a stock pot and add another quart of water and let simmer for at least 6 hours. Now strain stock

through colander into saucepan. Reduce stock to 3 cups. Let cool, refrigerate overnight. Next day, skim off the fat of stock. Now you can make the sauce at your convenience.

Sauce:

To make a good sauce, you need 3 basic ingredients. Stock, roux, and seasoning. There should be approximately 3 cups of stock which should be heated up. To make your roux, warm up a 2-quart saucepan over medium heat. Add 4 tablespoons of shortening and 5 tablespoons of all-purpose flour. Stir until golden brown. Remove from heat and let cool for a few minutes. Pour in stock, stirring vigorously. Put back on heat. Bring to a boil. Turn down heat and let simmer for at least a half an hour until sauce thickens. Now strain through fine strainer to remove any lumps.

With vegetable peeler, peel off just the outer zest of an orange. Then cut the zest into very thin juliennes. Add 4 ounces orange juice concentrate. Add the orange zest, salt to taste, pinch of ground cloves, pinch of ground cardamom, pinch of ground ginger, 2 ounces Grand Marnier, and 1 ounce of Cognac. Add 2 tablespoons of Kitchen Bouquet. Just let simmer for 1 more minute and remove from heat.

Sweet Potato:

1 lb. fresh sweet potatoes
1 small tart apple
1 Tbsp. butter
juice of ½ lemon
2 Tbsps. sugar
1 small can sliced pineapple
1 pinch ground cinnamon
1 pinch ground ginger
1 pinch ground cloves
1 pinch ground cardamom

Peel and dice sweet potato and apple. Simmer over low to medium heat in covered saucepan until tender, with butter, lemon juice, the juice of the pineapple and sugar. Stir frequently to make sure it doesn't burn. When tender, remove from heat and let cool. Mash to a puree. Pipe through a pastry bag on top of four pineapple slices. Place on a greased baking sheet. When ready to serve place duck and sweet potato in a 350 degree preheated oven for 10-12 minutes. Heat sauce. When ready to serve, garnish with slices of fresh orange.

From: **Bernard's**
Continental Restaurant
North Second Street
Stevens Point, Wisconsin

Roast Breast of Goose

2 1½-lb. goose breasts
salt & pepper
1 qt. chicken stock
1 sliced onion
1 peeled & chunked carrot
1 tsp. honey
1 cup white wine
roux*

Preheat oven to 450 degrees. Season breasts with salt and pepper. Place in baking pan and bake 35 minutes until well browned. Remove from oven and pour off fat, reserving for later use.

To the browned breasts, add onion, carrot, honey, wine and chicken stock. Return to oven, covering pan. Braise for 1-1½ hours until fork tender.

Remove breasts to serving platter and keep warm. Strain drippings and stock and remove vegetables, skimming as much fat as possible off the stock. Add to the saucepan.

Bring stock to simmer and gradually add roux until correct consistency is achieved.

Slice goose to serving size. Pour sauce over and serve immediately.

Roux:
¼ cup reserved goose fat
¾ cup flour

Heat goose fat, add flour, a little at a time until smooth, the texture of sour cream. Constantly stirring, cook 2-3 minutes over low heat.

From: **The Fox and Hounds**
1298 Freiss Lake Road
Hubertus, Wisconsin

Hungarian Goulash

2 lbs. beef chuck,
   cut into large chunks
2 lbs. onions, about 5 cups
1 bay leaf
2 oz. salad oil
1 tsp. tomato puree
1 quart beef stock
a little salt
1½ tsps. Hungarian paprika

Lemon paste:
1 tsp. lemon rind
1 small clove garlic
1 tsp. caraway seed

Brown meat and season to taste with salt. After browning well, add onions, bay leaf, salad oil and continue cooking. Add beef stock, tomato puree, and paprika. Simmer gently for about 1 hour. Add lemon paste and cook until tender for 2 hours. To make the lemon paste crush garlic clove, put lemon rind and caraway seed on top of clove and chop with a knife until a paste. Water can be added during this last cooking process as needed. If more gravy is needed, add a tablespoon of flour, which you have mixed with water and simmer a few minutes, then add more water. But a "Gulyas Naturel" without any flour is of course the real thing. Serve with boiled potatoes, noodles or dumplings. A very good way to eat a "Gulyas" is just with a fresh, crisp roll.

From: **Mader's**
1037 North Third Street
Milwaukee, Wisconsin

Braised Beef Roll-Up

2 lbs. round, rib or
*   top sirloin*
salt & pepper
dark mustard
¼ lb. bacon
2 dill pickles
1 onion
3 Tbsps. flour
½ cup sour cream

Rinse meat, remove membrane, cut across the grain into flat steaks, pound with a dampened meat hammer. Salt and spread thinly with mustard. Cut bacon and dill pickles into strips. Chop onion. Place bacon, pickle and onion on each steak, sprinkle with pepper, roll tightly, and fasten with a toothpick. Dredge each steak with flour. Heat fat in a skillet. Brown steaks on all sides. Place well-browned steaks with fat into a saucepan, add a little water and stew, covered until tender. Mix remaining flour with sour cream, add to meat, add salt to taste. Bring to a boil. Serve.

From: **Cracovia Restaurant**
1531 West Lincoln Avenue
Milwaukee, Wisconsin

Pork Fremont

1 5-6 lb. boneless center cut
   pork loin
2 lbs. Kalberwurst
2 tsps. white pepper
2/3 cup Calvados apple brandy
4 cups mushrooms, diced
1 lb. Westphalian ham,
   sliced very thin
1 bunch green onions
Calvados Cream Sauce

Slit skin of Kalberwurst and remove. Mix Kalberwurst, pepper, Calvados, and mushrooms thoroughly.

Cut pork loin, starting at tail, ¾" thick so you can lay it out as a rectangle. Imagine the process backwards as in a jellyroll.

Layer Westphalian ham over meat, spread Kalberwurst mixture over that and set green onions lengthwise at intervals. Roll back up jelly roll fashion and tie. Season with salt and pepper. Roast at 350 degrees to an internal temperature of 160 degrees, or about 1½ hours. Remove from pan. Pour off fat. Measure juices and add cider to make 1½ cups. Return to roasting pan and heat. Scrape up all the little brown bits. In a saucepan over medium heat, mix fat and flour to make a roux. Cook two minutes, whisking. Add pan juices and continue to cook and whisk until smooth and thick. Add the Calvados and cream. Slice pork loin and serve with the sauce.

Calvados Cream Sauce:
½ cup pan juices
1 cup cider
2 Tbsps. pork fat
3 Tbsps. flour
4 Tbsps. cream
4 Tbsps. Calvados

From: **Quivey's Grove**
6261 Nesbit Road
Madison, Wisconsin

Tenderloin Madeira

4 6-8 oz. tenderloin filets

Marinade:
5 cups beef stock
6 cloves minced garlic
1 tsp. thyme
3 cups Madeira wine
1 tsp. white pepper
¼ cup minced parsley

Method:
Let tenderloin stand in marinade for at least 8 hours. Saute the meat in butter until doneness desired. While meat is sauteeing, strain the marinade and put in a pan and reduce it over high heat until it becomes a slightly thickened glaze. The meat and sauce will take about the same for a medium cooked steak. Pour a little of the sauce on each steak. Meat may be broiled as well.

From: **The Ovens of Brittany
—Monroe Street**
1831 Monroe Street
Madison, Wisconsin

Beef Wellington

6 6-oz. beef tenderloin steaks
2 ozs. ham
8 ozs. fresh mushrooms, cleaned
1 small onion, peeled
½ clove garlic, peeled
1 Tbsp. chopped parsley
6 8" sheets puff pastry
1 egg, beaten
butter, salt, pepper, flour

Brown steaks in butter or margarine for 1½ minutes on each side in hot frying pan. Cool.

Grind ham, mushrooms, onion and garlic together and saute in butter for 5 minutes. Thicken with a little flour and season to taste with salt and pepper. Add parsley. Cool.

Cut puff pastry in 8" squares. Place 1 tablespoon of mushroom mixture in center of each square. Place steak on top of mixture and top with another tablespoon of mixture. Fold the pastry up so that the steak is completely wrapped. Place Wellingtons, seam side down, on a baking sheet and brush with beaten egg.

Bake at 375 degrees for 25-30 minutes, or

until pastry is golden brown. The steaks should come out medium to medium rare. Spoon ½ cup of Madeira sauce on a heated plate and top with Wellington. Yield: 6 servings.

Note: For a decorative touch, cut star- or heart-shaped pieces out of the leftover pastry and place atop Wellingtons before baking.

From: **Barth's at the Bridge**
N58 W6194 Columbia Road
Cedarburg, Wisconsin

Madeira Sauce

1 Tbsp. chopped ham
2 Tbsps. butter
1 small carrot
1 small onion
1 stalk celery
2 Tbsps. flour
2 cups brown stock
2 tomatoes
1 small bay leaf
3 peppercorns
1 sprig parsley
½ sprig thyme
1 garlic clove
1 cup Madeira

Cook the chopped ham in the butter for a few minutes. Add the carrots, onions, and celery, all chopped, and cook briskly, stirring constantly, until the vegetables are brown. Stir in flour and brown it. Add the brown stock and the remaining vegetables and herbs, cook, stirring, until the sauce thickens. Cook slowly for 20 minutes. Remove the fat that rises to the surface during cooking. Strain the sauce and discard the vegetables. The sauce will be as thick as cream. Finish the sauce with the Madeira, and heat it without boiling. Adjust the seasoning with salt and pepper and serve.

From: **Barth's at the Bridge**
N58 W56194 Columbia Road
Cedarburg, Wisconsin

Marinade for Lamb Shishkebabs

2 cups vegetable oil
½ cup dried mint leaves
¾ cup red wine vinegar
5 cloves of garlic, minced
¼ cup fresh lemon juice

Combine all ingredients and mix well.

Trim fat and gristle from lamb legs. Cut into 1-2" pieces. Place in marinade for at least 24 hours, preferably 48. Skewer meat alternating wtih fresh vegetables. Grill, brushing with marinade as you cook.

From: **The Red Geranium**
Hwy. E
Lake Geneva, Wisconsin

Veal Tenderloin Medallions
with Green Peppercorn Cream Sauce

2 filets of veal
¾ cup heavy cream
20 green peppercorns
½ cup red wine, sherry or port

This recipe serves 2. Multiply as needed.

Preheat a tall-sided saucepan until very hot. Sear filets on both sides for three minutes or until well browned over high heat, in a buttered pan. (I use a slight amount of butter in the pan to start instead of oil because I feel oil doesn't compliment the flavor). Steak will fry nicely without the heavy use of oil and butter. If the steak sticks to the pan while frying, slide a metal spatula underneath to release.

Remove the browned filets from pan and pour in ½ cup red wine, cream sherry or port and reduce the volume by half. Add the heavy

cream and continue to continue to reduce. Add 20 green peppercorns and return the filets to the pan, rewarming in the sauce.

Place the filets on a plate and pour the sauce over top. Serve.

From: **The Jamieson House**
Poynette, Wisconsin

Count Esterhazy Schnitzel

2 Tbsps. butter
1 clove garlic
½ cup finely diced onions
1 bay leaf
5 cups sliced mushrooms
3 cups veal stock
½ cup roux (little less)
1½ cups sour cream
8 3-oz. veal cutlets
seasoned flour

Place butter in saucepan. Slightly crush clove of garlic and saute in butter so you get a little garlic flavor. Take out garlic clove and add onions. Saute onions but do not brown. Add bay leaf. When onions are lightly sauteed add sliced mushrooms and cook until done. In a separate pot bring stock to boil and add roux. Cook until smooth. Strain thickened stock into mushrooms and bring to a boil. Take a small portion of mushroom sauce and add to sour cream stirring rapidly to avoid curdling. Blend this with the rest of the mushroom sauce and keep warm. Do not boil once sour cream has been added.

Dust veal cutlets in seasoned flour and saute in clarified butter. Cook veal and place on plate. Dab off excess butter. Spoon desired amount of Esterhazy sauce over veal and serve with buttered noodles or spaetzle.

From: **Mader's**
1037 North Third Street
Milwaukee, Wisconsin

Veal Scallopini

6 oz. veal, preferably in
    2 oz. leg slices
2 Tbsps. olive oil
1 cup chicken stock
½ cup sliced fresh mushrooms
¼ cup chopped shallots
few drops Kitchen Bouquet

Dust veal in flour and over medium high heat, saute in olive oil. Remove from pan and keep warm. Add chicken stock to pan and add mushrooms and shallots. Cook until tender. Add Kitchen Bouquet to taste and color, bring to a boil and thicken to a thin sauce. Add veal to reheat and serve immediately.

We use Provimi veal and have had the best results. Garnish.

From: **Florena Supper Club**
N3380 Hwy. 13
Medford, Wisconsin

Escalope de Veau Christine

2 4-oz. escalopes of veal
butter
finely diced onions
salt & pepper
cream
Sherry
Lea & Perrins
    Worcestershire sauce
Cognac

Place 1 teaspoon butter in pan and melt.

Add onions, 1 teaspoon. When onions soften, add escalopes and cook approximately 2 minutes on each side.

While veal is cooking, add salt and pepper. Transfer escalopes to another pan, in butter.

Add ½ serving spoon of cream to the pan in which the veal was cooked.

Add 1 glass sherry and 1 teaspoon Lea & Perrins.

While the sauce is heating, add Cognac to

the veal and flame.

Extinquish veal by pouring sauce over veal. Place on serving plate and garnish with parsley. Serve.*

*Preferably with noodles.

From:

Bailey's Harbor Yacht Club
Bailey's Harbor, Wisconsin

Veal with Morel Sauce

12 2-oz veal scallops
flour, nutmeg, ground
thyme, ground bay leaf
clarified butter
12 ozs. morel mushrooms,
  cleaned and cut ½ if large
1 cup veal stock
1 cup heavy cream
3 ozs. Madeira

Dredge veal in seasoned flour. Heat about 4 tablespoons clarified butter over medium high heat in large skillet. Saute veal 1½ minutes on one side, turn, add mushrooms and saute 1½ minutes till medium rare. Remove veal to platter and keep warm. Turn heat high and add stock. Reduce by half. Add cream and boil until sauce will coat a spoon. Stir in Madeira and serve over veal.

From:

Quivey's Grove
6261 Nesbit Road
Madison, Wisconsin

Wiener Schnitzel

2 lbs. veal roast, sliced
  ¼" thick, approx. 3 oz. slices
dash of garlic
1 Tbsp. salt
½ tsp. white pepper
¼ tsp. paprika

1 cup flour
1 egg
1 cup milk
2 cups bread crumbs
½ cup shortening

For Emmanthal variation:
Swiss cheese
ham

Season each slice of veal with salt, white pepper paprika and garlic. Pound each piece of veal until nice and even.

Flour each slice of veal, dip into egg wash made of egg beaten with the cup of milk, then dip into bread crumbs. Melt shortening in a large skillet, saute veal slowly until golden brown and tender.

For Emmanthal:

Take two slices of wiener schnitzel, add a slice of ham ⅛" thick to cover and a slice of Swiss cheese on top of the ham. Bake in the oven until cheese melts.

Note: Emmanthal means cheese so you can use any kind of cheese.

From: **The Golden Mast Inn**
1270 Lacy's Lane
Okauchee, Wisconsin

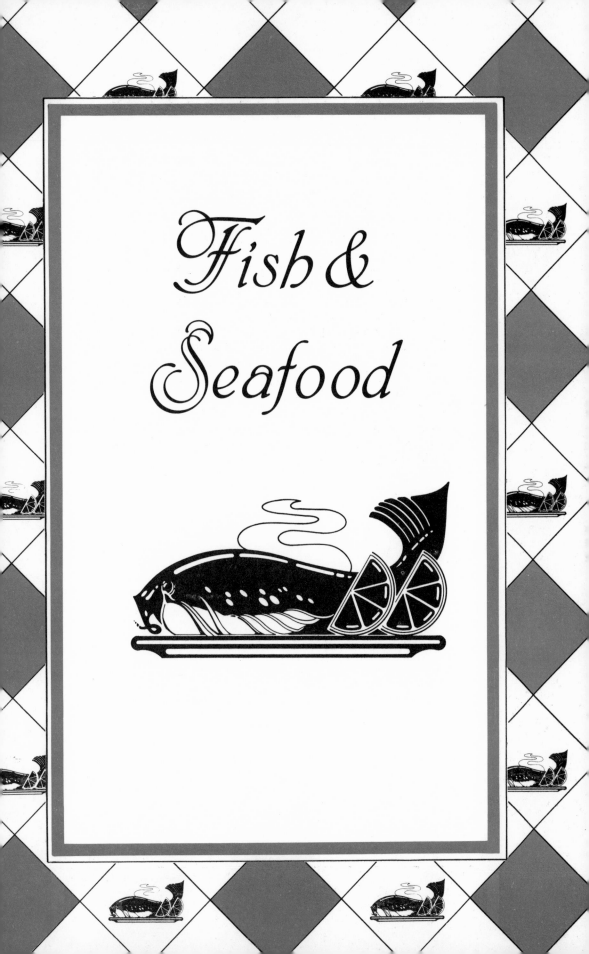

Fish & Seafood

Fish & Seafood

Wisconsin's borders are water to a great extent and the interior rich with lakes, rivers and streams. People here are used to eating fish, it has always been a part of the local diet.

What has changed is the use of seafood both at home and in restaurants. Seafood this far inland used to consist only of oysters which could be packed in barrels and kept "fresh" for a couple of months. Now the shrimp, lobster, swordfish, mussels, clams and other delicacies from the sea, are put on a plane and here in a matter of hours. Wisconsin's chefs are having as much fun with that as chefs anywhere.

Poached Salmon
in Mousseline Sauce
with Kiwi Fruit & Red Lump Caviar

4 8-oz. Sockeye salmon filets

Poaching Liquid:
6 Tbsps. butter
1 cup chopped onion
1 cup chopped carrot
1 cup chopped celery
1½ cups dry white wine
1 bay leaf
1 Tbsp. cracked black
  peppercorns

Mousseline Sauce:
½ pt. heavy cream
4 egg yolks
¼ tsp. cayenne
¼ tsp. salt
½ tsp. Worcestershire sauce
juice of 1 lemon
½ lb. butter, cut up

In a large saucepan, saute the onion, carrot, and celery in butter over moderately high heat for 5 minutes. Add 12 cups water and the bay leaf and cracked pepper and the wine and simmer for 20 minutes. Strain liquid. Reheat liquid and poach salmon in liquid for 5-8 minutes. Remove salmon from poaching liquid, remove skin, transfer to plate and keep warm.

In a chilled bowl, whip the heavy cream until thick and set aside. In the top half of double boiler, place the egg yolks and 4 tablespoons of water and whip until smooth. Add the pepper, salt, Worcestershire, and lemon juice and whip in all the butter, 1 piece at a time. Remove from the heat and let stand for 10 minutes.

Fold whipped cream into Hollandaise and divide onto 4 serving plates. Place salmon on sauce. Garnish each filet with 2 slices of Kiwi fruit topped with caviar. Serve immediately. Yield: 4 servings.

From: **Carver's on the Lake**
799 Inlet Road
Green Lake, Wisconsin

Gulf Shrimp Maureen

butter
shrimp
dry vermouth
salt & pepper
brandy
fresh cream

Melt butter in round frying pan. When melted, add shrimp and cook approximately 3 minutes. Add 2 ounces vermouth and the juice of ½ lime. Salt and pepper to taste. Add brandy and flame. Extinguish flame with cream. Serve on bed of rice garnished with green peppers. Yield: 1 serving.

From: **Bailey's Harbor
Yacht Club**
Bailey's Harbor, Wisconsin

Coquilles St. Jacques Parisienne

2 lbs. fresh sea scallops
3 cups dry white wine
seasoning salt
fresh lemon juice
1 qt. natural heavy cream
   (do not use "whipping" cream)
white pepper

Poach scallops in wine until firm, about 3-4 minutes. Remove the scallops from the wine and set aside. Add the cream to the wine with a dash of the seasoning salt and a dash of the white pepper and a drop of the lemon juice.

Bring to a boil, reduce to a simmer. Simmer the sauce until reduced, about 15-20 minutes. Sauce will be thick and smooth and should be a buttery yellow color.

Using a different pan, add the scallops back into the sauce. Heat through, divide into scallop shells, pipe with Duchesse potatoes and serve.

Duchesse Potatoes:
4 cups riced potatoes
2 egg yolks, beaten
dash dry mustard
¼ cup butter
dash salt & pepper to taste

Add the eggs, mustard, butter and salt and pepper to the potatoes. Put in pastry tube and flute decoratively around the edges of the shells containing the Coquilles.

From: **The Fess Hotel**
123 Doty Street
Madison, Wisconsin

Cajun Barbecue Shrimp

Seasoning Blend:
2 tsps. cayenne pepper
1 tsp. salt
1 tsp. thyme
1 tsp. rosemary
2 tsps. ground black pepper
½ tsp. coarsely ground
  black pepper
¼ tsp. oregano

2 Tbsps. clarified butter
1 clove garlic, chopped fine
1 tsp. seasoning blend
¼ tsp. Worcestershire
4 10/15 count shrimp
¼ cup beer

Combine all the ingredients for the seasoning blend.

Split shrimp on the belly side.

In saute pan, melt the clarified butter, add garlic, seasoning blend, Worcestershire sauce. Heat over medium flame, stirring to blend. Add shrimp, meat side down. Saute. Turn heat to medium high for only a minute or two. Turn shrimp to shell side. Add ¼ cup beer. Cover pan and turn off heat.

From: **Faller's**
Seafood Restaurant
The Rennaissance Inn
414 Maple Drive
Sister Bay, Wisconsin

Bayou Crawfish Etoufee
(A-TOO-FAY—Cajun French for "Smothered in Sauce")

3 cups white onion, chopped fine
¼ cup parsley, chopped fine
2 ozs. sweet butter

8 ozs. sweet butter
⅔ cup whole wheat pastry
or unbleached flour
2 cups half & half
1 cup milk
1½ cups white wine
½ tsp. garlic salt
3 ozs. tomato paste
2 dashes tabasco
1 lb. crawfish tails
sea salt to taste

4 cups natural brown rice,
cooked

You will need 10 pounds of whole crawfish to yield 1 pound of tail meat. Fill a large pot half up with water. Add one bag of shrimp and crab boil seasoning, ½ cup sea salt and ½ cup cayenne pepper. Bring water to a high boil for five minutes. Add 10 pounds of live crawfish. Bring back to a boil until crawfish turn red. Shut off heat and let crawfish set in pot for a few minutes. Remove from pot and peel out tail meat. Save. (Crawfish tails are now being sold by the pound in some of your finer specialty stores. They are frozen and their taste is almost as good as fresh.)

Saute onions, parsley and 2 ounces sweet butter until onions are clear. Set aside.

In a large pan, place 8 ounces of sweet butter, flour and make into a light roux. Add cream, milk and cook into a cream sauce. Then add wine and cook until smooth. Add all other ingredients, including sauteed onions and crawfish tails and cook over a low heat until ingredients have blended together. Keep a watchful eye and stir often to avoid burning sauce. A double boiler can be used if you wish. Serve over rice with French bread and a semi-dry white wine. Yield: 4-6 entrees or 8 appetizer servings.

From: **The Blue Bayou Inn**
Manitowish Waters, Wisconsin

Swordfish Dijonnaise

6 8-oz. pieces swordfish ¾" thick
Dijon mustard
salt & pepper to taste
white bread crumbs
clarified butter
Beurre Blanc Sauce

Season swordfish steaks with salt and pepper to your own taste. Brush in Dijon mustard and coat with bread crumbs. Saute in clarified butter for 3 minutes on low heat. Drain on paper towels. Pour Beurre Blanc Sauce on plate to cover lightly and place swordfish on top. Garnish of your choice.

Beurre Blanc Sauce:
3 shallots, finely chopped
4 Tbsps. white wine
2 Tbsps. white vinegar
1 Tbsp. Dijon mustard
6 ozs. sweet butter
1 Tbsp. fresh dill

For sauce, combine shallots, wine and vinegar in saucepan. Bring to a boil and cook until reduced to 3 tablespoons. Remove from heat and add mustard. Whisk in softened butter 1 piece at a time, blending completely. Season with salt and pepper to taste. Add dill last.

From: **Grenadier's Restaurant**
747 North Broadway
Milwaukee, Wisconsin

Garided Tourkolimano
(Greek Shrimp)

30 green shrimp,
  peeled & deveined
lemon juice
touch of garlic powder
2 cups whipped butter
1 cup chopped green onion tips
3 lg. tomatoes,
  cored & cut into 8 wedges each
salt & pepper to taste
2 tsps. leaf oregano
1 lb. feta cheese
6 ozs. cream sherry

Pour lemon juice over cleaned shrimp and set aside. Blend garlic powder in butter. In a skillet, melt butter and saute green onion tips and tomato wedges. Add shrimp to skillet mixture. Add salt and pepper. Sprinkle with oregano. Turn shrimp frequently and saute until pink. Add crumbled feta cheese and cream sherry. Remove shrimp with spoon so that melted feta stays intact, and place in casserole. Spoon liquid mixture over shrimp. Serve with rice pilaf. Yield: 6 servings.

From: **Michael's Restaurant**
1815 Ward Avenue
LaCrosse, Wisconsin

Sweet Basil Shrimp

8 lg. shrimp, peeled
3 ozs. white wine
sea salt to taste
½ cup cooked natural brown rice
2 ozs. sweet butter
1 tsp. sweet basil leaves
dash tabasco sauce

Place all ingredients into saute pan except rice. Saute until shrimp are half cooked. Cover pan and remove from heat. Let set for 5 minutes. Shrimp will finish cooking without overcooking, (use this method of cooking shrimp for other shrimp dishes you may have). Serve over hot rice with French bread

and a glass of dry or semi-dry white wine.
Yield: 1 entree or 4 appetizer servings.

From: **The Blue Bayou Inn**
Manitowish Waters, Wisconsin

Grilled Salmon Steak Choron

4 11-12-oz. Atlantic
   salmon steaks
4 ozs. clarified butter
1 Tbsp. fresh lemon juice
1 tsp. Lawry's seasoning salt
½ tsp. black pepper
½ tsp. Hungarian paprika
1 cup water

1 cup sauce Bearnaise
4 tsps. fried bread crumbs
1 Tbsp. tomato paste

Sear salmon steaks on both sides of grill. Place them in a shallow roasting pan. Pour butter and lemon juice over fish. Season fish with seasoning salt, black pepper, and paprika. Pour water in roasting pan. Bake at 450 degrees for 25 minutes or until fish is done.

Mix tomato paste with Bearnaise sauce. Serve 3 ounces of sauce over each steak and sprinkle with fried bread crumbs.

From: **Karl Ratzsch's**
320 East Mason Street
Milwaukee, Wisconsin

Salmon with Morels and Cream

¾ cup Madeira
5 cups heavy cream
1 pound fresh morels
  or 2-3 ozs. dried
clarified butter
6 5-6-oz. pieces of skinless
  salmon fillet
salt, white pepper & cayenne
  to taste

In a 2-quart enamel or stainless steel saucepan, reduce Madeira over a gentle heat until 3 tablespoons remain. Add the heavy cream and the morels and again reduce the mixture until 2-2½ cups remain.

Preheat oven to 475 degrees. Brush a baking pan with some of the clarified butter. Arrange the salmon fillets on the buttered baking pan and brush them with more of the clarified butter. Bake in the upper half of the oven for 6-9 minutes, or until the fish is tender and will gently "flake."

Season the sauce to taste with the salt, white pepper and cayenne. Mask the fillets with the sauce and serve. Yield: 6 servings.

From: **L'Etoile**
                    25 N. Pinckney
                 Madison, Wisconsin

Salads &

Salad

Dressings

Salads & Salad Dressings

There is an almost endless diversity to salads, what you can make them out of and how you can dress them. Salads can be a course to cleanse the palate during an elaborate dinner, they can be something simple and delicious eaten in haste and they can be a meal all by themselves.

Here are some of each for you to try.

Marinated Vegetable Salad

Vegetables:
green or red bell peppers,
cut into thin strips
garbanzo beans
celery, cut on the diagonal
red onion, cut into thin strips
green onions, chopped
artichoke hearts, quartered
carrots, thinly sliced
broccoli flowerettes, blanched
cauliflower pieces, blanched
cherry tomatoes
sliced, fresh mushrooms
black or green olives, pitted

Herbs:
parsley, dill, lemon thyme, mint,
chives, Greek oregano, basil,
fennel, etc.

You can "mix and match" the ingredients to this salad to fit the season or your taste-buds. Choose 5 or 6 vegetables in equal parts. You will need about 1 tablespoon fresh chopped herbs for every 3 cups of vegetables. Toss the salad with a good vinaigrette dressing, enough to coat the vegetables very well. Add salt and freshly ground pepper to taste. Let the salad marinate several hours in the refrigerator, tossing often. Serve as a first course or to accompany meats, fish or poultry.

From: **The Ovens of Brittany —East**
1718 Fordem Road
Madison, Wisconsin

Oriental Cole Slaw

4 quarts shredded cole slaw
3 ozs. sliced, canned mushrooms, drained
1 Tbsp. finely chopped onion
½ cup mayonnaise
1 Tbsp. soy sauce
½ cup chow mein noodles

Combine cabbage, mushrooms, and onion. Blend together mayonnaise and soy sauce. Toss lightly with cabbage mixture. Just before serving, top with noodles. Yield: 6-8 servings.

From: **Michael's Restaurant**
1815 Ward Avenue
LaCrosse, Wisconsin

Saloon Slaw

4 cups sugar
1 cup water
2 cups white vinegar
1 Tbsp. salt

1 large head cabbage
2 green peppers
1 bunch celery

2 Tbsps. celery seed
2 Tbsps. mustard seed

Boil the first four ingredients for 15 minutes and set aside to cool. Shred the cabbage coarsely in the food processor. Cut up the peppers and celery finely and add to the cabbage and mix the mustard and celery seed in. Pour in cooled liquid and transfer to an airtight container. This can be kept refrigerated for up to 6 weeks. Refrigerate at least 8 hours before serving.

From: **The Star Lake Saloon and Eatery**
Starlake, Wisconsin

Bombay Salad

8 apples, unpeeled, sliced thinly
½ cup sugar
½ cup fresh lime juice
½ cup sliced almonds
4 cups plain yogurt
   (Nancy's or other good natural)
1 Tbsp. curry powder
½ cup unsweetened coconut

Combine the above ingredients and toss gently. Chill. Serve on a bed of leaf lettuce.

From: **The Fess Hotel**
          129 Doty Street
          Madison, Wisconsin

Curried Chicken Salad

2½ cups pineapple chunks
3½ oz. pimento
1½ scallions, chopped
1 cup celery, chopped
1½ cups mayonnaise
1½ tsps. curry powder
1½ tsps. turmeric
½ lb. cooked breast of chicken,
   shredded
cashews for garnish

Drain pineapple, put in bowl. Drain pimento and dice, add to pineapple. Add chopped scallions, celery and mayonnaise. Mix thoroughly. Add curry, turmeric, blending completely. Add shredded chicken. Serve on a bed of lettuce and alfalfa sprouts. Garnish with cashews.

From: **The Cafe Palms**
          636 West Washington Avenue
          Madison, Wisconsin

Tenderloin Spinach Salad

8 ozs. cubed tenderloin
2 Tbsps. butter
1 Tbsp. Worcestershire
1 Tbsp. garlic salt
2 Tbsps. green onions, chopped
¼ cup sliced, fresh mushrooms
dash chopped parsley
2 Tbsps. Parmesan cheese
1 bag fresh, cleaned spinach
¼ cup sliced black olives.

Saute tenderloin in butter. Add Worcestershire sauce, garlic salt, green onions, mushrooms, parsley and add Parmesan last. Saute until tenderloin is medium rare.

Serve on a bed of fresh spinach with bleu cheese dressing on the side. Also may be garnished with more Parmesan cheese and sliced black olives.

From: **The Vintage House**
Hwy. 13 North
Wisconsin Rapids, Wisconsin

Wild Rice, Peas and Mushroom Salad

½ lb. mushrooms, thinly sliced
juice of 1 lemon
½ lb. wild rice, cooked & drained
2 cups fresh green peas,
   cooked & drained
4 green onions, thinly sliced
¾ cup vinaigrette
1 Tbsp. finely chopped
   fresh tarragon or
   ¼ tsp. dried, crumbled
¼ tsp. sugar

Combine mushrooms and lemon juice in large bowl. Add rice, peas and onion. Combine vinaigrette, tarragon and sugar in small bowl and mix well. Add to rice mixture. Toss lightly. Season with salt and pepper to taste.

Vinaigrette

1 small to medium garlic clove,
   minced
2 tsps. Dijon mustard
1 tsp. coarse salt
½ tsp. freshly ground pepper,
   or to taste
¼ cup white wine vinegar
⅓-½ cup oil

Combine garlic, mustard, salt and pepper in medium bowl. Slowly whisk in vinegar. Gradually add oil, whisking constantly until thoroughly blended.

From: **The Stockpot**
1730 Fordem Road
Madison, Wisconsin

Marinated Mushroom Salad

1 lb. fresh mushrooms

Marinade:
⅔ cup olive oil
½ tsp. sugar
1 tsp. Worcestershire sauce
1 Tbsp. minced onion
1 tsp. paprika
1 egg yolk
½ cup chili sauce
½ cup cider vinegar
½ tsp. leaf tarragon
1 tsp. prepared mustard
*½ tsp. freshly, finely
    chopped garlic*
1 Tbsp. lemon juice
½ bottle (7 oz.) ketchup
salt to taste

For marinade combine all ingredients and mix well.

Clean and thinly slice 1 pound fresh mushrooms. Toss with the marinade and allow to rest overnight in covered container. (Shaking the container once or twice through the marinating process helps.)

Pour mushroom mixture through strainer, saving liquid for future use.

Add 2 tablespoons chopped chives and 2 tablespoons finely chopped sweet, red pepper.

May be served as is, or spooned atop leaf lettuce and garnished with hard cooked egg slices.

From: **The Fox and Hounds**
1298 Freiss Lake Road
Hubertus, Wisconsin

Autumn Salad

½ tsp. minced garlic
dash sea salt
peppercorns
2 Tbsps. Champagne vinegar
4 Tbsps. good olive oil
1 head romaine lettuce,
    cleaned, ribbed & broken into
    serving pieces, patted dry
⅓ cup minced chives
1½ cups quartered yellow & red
    cherry tomatoes
⅓ cup pomegranate seeds
⅔ cup julienne of fresh pear

Mince garlic in mortar with sea salt and peppercorns. Add vinegar, mix with whip, now slowly add oil, beating as you go. Toss lettuce, chives, and salad dressing in a chilled bowl. Add tomatoes and pomegranate seeds. Garnish with fresh pear. Yield: 6 servings.

From: **Chez Michel**
7601 Mineral Point Road
Madison, Wisconsin

Bernard's House Dressing

1 pint sour cream
½ cup oil
½ cup vinegar
1 Tbsp. onion powder
1 Tbsp. sugar
¼ tsp. garlic powder
1 Tbsp. salt
1 Tbsp. dill weed
½ tsp. pepper
½ tsp. ground oregano

Whip sour cream in mixer and slowly add the oil. Continue whipping and add vinegar and spices. Yield: 1 quart.

From: **Bernard's**
Continental Restaurant
North Second Street
Stevens Point, Wisconsin

Ginger Vinaigrette

1 egg
dash white pepper
1 tsp. dry mustard
½ tsp. salt
1½ Tbsps. sugar
1 tsp. paprika
2 cups salad oil
½ cup red wine vinegar
½ tsp. Worcestershire
2½ Tbsps. lemon juice
1 tsp. freshly grated ginger root

Beat egg until thickened. Add dry ingredients to eggs and blend well. Add oil 1 drop at a time until mixture begins to thicken. Begin adding the vinegar and remaining oil slowly, alternating until ingredients are used up. Add the Worcestershire sauce and lemon juice. Add freshly grated ginger root.

From: **The Red Geranium**
          Hwy. 50E
          Lake Geneva, Wisconsin

Cucumber Yogurt Dressing

1½ medium cucumbers,
   cut in chunks & seeded
   (2 if small)
1 cup oil
1 tsp. dill
¼ tsp. salt & pepper
1 clove garlic
1 cup plain yogurt
1 cup sour cream
⅓ cup vinegar
1 cup parsley

Blend all ingredients thoroughly.

From: **The Sunprint**
          Cafe and Gallery
          638 State Street
          Madison, Wisconsin

Tarragon and Mustard Vinaigrette

1 Tbsp. Dijon mustard
½ cup cider vinegar
1 Tbsp. sugar
1 tsp. dried tarragon
1 clove garlic, finely chopped
1 whole egg
salt & freshly ground pepper
    to taste
1 cup oil

Combine first seven ingredients and blend well. Stir in oil, a little at a time and blend well. Let sit for 12 hours.

From: **Carver's on the Lake**
799 Inlet Road
Green Lake, Wisconsin

Raspberry Vinaigrette

1 cup oil
¼ cup fresh or frozen raspberries
    (availability)
salt & sugar to taste
½ cup raspberry vinegar*
¼ tsp. whole black peppercorns

Place all ingredients except salt and sugar in blender and blend at high speed. Add salt and sugar to taste. If you allow vinaigrette to sit over a period of time, it will separate and must be re-blended.
*We use Vinaigre de Vin a l'Ancienne a la Framboise, Martin Pouret-Orleans France.

From: **The Cafe Palms**
636 West Washington Avenue
Madison, Wisconsin

Lemon Dijon Dressing

¼ cup + 1 Tbsp. sugar
1 Tbsp. salt
3 Tbsps. fresh lemon juice
2 Tbsps. white vinegar
¼ cup Dijon Grey Poupon
   mustard*
1 clove garlic, chopped very fine
25 turns freshly ground pepper
1½ cups oil
1 egg yolk

Dissolve the sugar and salt in the lemon juice and vinegar. Mix in the mustard, garlic and pepper. Whisk in the oil, a little at a time. Add 1 egg yolk and whisk with wire whip. Refrigerate for 1 hour and whisk again until thick and creamy.

*Do not substitute as proper results will not be achieved.

From:

**Inn of the
Four Seasons**
Hwy. 99 and County E
Eagle, Wisconsin

Cheddar Cheese Dressing

1 tsp. lemon juice
1 tsp. Worcestershire sauce
2 Tbsps. chives
1 pint sour cream
¼ cup half & half
1 tsp. dry mustard
1 Tbsp. minced onion
½ tsp. tabasco
1 Tbsp. sugar
1 tsp. garlic salt
4 ozs. sharp Cheddar cheese,
   grated fine

Put all ingredients into a bowl and whip together. Refrigerate at least a day for flavors to blend. Use on salads, potatoes, or as a dip.

From:

Quivey's Grove
6261 Nesbit Road
Madison, Wisconsin

Hot Bacon Dressing

3 slices bacon
1 Tbsp. onion, diced
1 Tbsp. sugar
1½ Tbsps. red wine vinegar
½ cup beef stock
½ cup chicken stock
1½ Tbsps. cornstarch
⅜ cup water

Fry bacon slices until crisp, remove and saute onions until transparent, draining off grease. Crumble bacon into pieces and add all ingredients together, except cornstarch and water. Bring to a boil. Combine cornstarch and water together and add slowly to boiling stock, thicken to desired consistency. Yield: Enough for 5-6 salads.

From: **The Golden Mast Inn**
1270 Lacy's Lane
Okauchee, Wisconsin

French Dressing

1 cup vegetable oil
¾ cup white vinegar
1 tsp. granulated onion
1 cup sugar
1 cup ketchup
1 Tbsp. Worcestershire sauce
1 Tbsp. salad mustard

Combine all ingredients in an electric blender. Blend on high speed for 1 minute. Let rest for 10 minutes and blend for another minute. Refrigerate for at least 3 hours before using. Can be stored in an airtight container in the refrigerator.

From: **The Star Lake
Saloon and Eatery**
Starlake, Wisconsin

SALADS & SALAD DRESSINGS

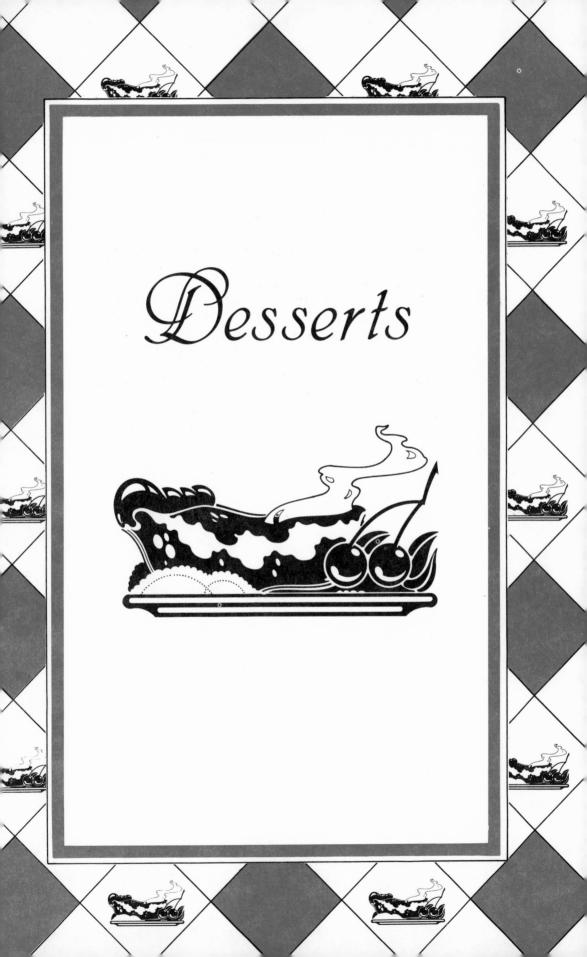

Desserts

Desserts

What can be said about desserts? A good dessert is a tribute to the meal that went before it, is a suitable ending to a wonderful meal.

Many of these recipes can also be eaten alone, as a special treat. They are so good that they can be eaten anytime, anywhere. Fresh fruits in abundance and maple syrup are local produce used. Chocolate is as popular in Wisconsin as it is anywhere. Heavy cream, butter and eggs pay tribute to our dairy and poultry industry.

From the number of desserts offered here, Wisconsin's sweet tooth is obviously in good hands.

Strawberry Wafer Torte

10 egg whites
½ tsp. almond extract
½ tsp. vanilla extract
3 cups blanched almonds, ground
1½ cups sugar
5 egg yolks
15 ozs. white chocolate, melted
½ cup + 2 Tbsps. butter,
    at room temperature
2 Tbsps. dark rum
4 Tbsps. white creme de cacao
    divided
2 Tbsps. fresh lime juice
⅔ cup strawberry jam
3 cups whipping cream, divided
¼ cup sugar
fresh strawberries for garnish

Beat egg whites until stiff peaks form. Beat in almond and vanilla extracts. Combine almonds with 1½ cups sugar. Fold almond mixture into the beaten egg whites. Spread mixture into five 8-9 inch circles on parchment paper lined cookie sheets. circles should be about ¼ inch thick. Bake in a pre-heated, 350 degree oven for about 20 to 30 minutes or until golden. Remove meringue wafers from oven and set aside on wire racks to cool. When wafers are cool, carefully remove them from the parchment paper. Set aside.

To make the filling, beat egg yolks until light and lemon colored. Add melted white chocolate. Mixture will be very thick and hard to stir. Mix in butter, rum, 2 tablespoons of creme de cacao, lime juice and strawberry jam. Mixture will lighten to the consistency of buttercream. Beat 1 cup whipping cream until stiff. Fold into white chocolate mixture. Set aside.

Spread white chocolate filling over 4 of the reserved meringue wafers. Stack wafers on top of one another neatly on a serving dish. Top with remaining wafer. (At this point torte can be wrapped and refrigerated for several hours. Bring to room temperature before frosting.)

To make the frosting, beat 2 cups whipping cream with ¼ cup sugar and 2 tablespoons of creme de cacao until stiff.

Spread whipped cream frosting on top and sides of wafer torte. If desired, reserve some frosting to pipe around top of torte. Garnish with strawberry halves arranged in a pretty pattern. Serve immediately. Yield: 12-16 servings.

From: **The Jamieson House**
Poynette, Wisconsin

Mississippi Mud Cake

2 cups sugar
1½ cups margarine
1 tsp. vanilla extract
⅓ cup cocoa
4 eggs

1½ cups flour
1½ cups chopped nuts
1⅓ cups coconut

Frosting:
½ cup margarine
½ cup milk
⅓ cup cocoa
2 cups powdered sugar
1 tsp. vanilla extract

Marshmallow cream

Mix together the sugar, cocoa, margarine and vanilla. Beat eggs and add to mixture. Mix together the flour, coconut, and nuts. Add to the first mixture, pour into a 9" x 13" pan and bake at 350 degrees for 40 minutes.

Spread one 7-ounce jar of marshmallow cream on cooled cake.

Put margarine, milk and cocoa into a pan and bring to a boil. Remove from heat and add the powdered sugar and vanilla. Beat well and spread on top of the marshmallow layer. Refrigerate. Yield: 1 rich sheet cake.

From: **The Mill Road Cafe**
Mill Road
Galesville, Wisconsin

Poppy Seed Torte

⅓ cup poppy seeds
1½ tsps. vanilla extract
¾ cup milk

¾ cup butter
1½ cups sugar
1¾ cups flour
2½ tsps. baking powder
1 tsp. salt
5 egg whites

Soak poppy seeds for one hour in ¾ cup milk. Add the vanilla.

Cream the butter and sugar, sift together the flour, baking powder and salt. Add to the creamed mixture. Fold in the stiffly beaten egg whites.

Bake in 2 well-greased, 8" round cake pans for 20-25 minutes at 375 degrees.

Cool 10 minutes, remove from pans and cool an additional 10 minutes. Split layers. Spread filling between layers and chill. Sift confectioner's sugar over the top.

Filling:
½ cup sugar
1 Tbsp. cornstarch
1½ cups milk
whipping cream
5 egg yolks, beaten
1 tsp. vanilla extract
¼ cup chopped nuts

For the filling, combine the sugar with cornstarch. Add the milk and egg yolks, beaten. Cook and stir until bubbling. Add the vanilla and the chopped nuts.

Cover the torte with whipped cream.

From: **The White Gull Inn**
Fish Creek, Wisconsin

German Sweet Chocolate Cake

4 ozs. German Sweet chocolate
½ cup boiling water
1 cup butter
2 cups sugar
4 egg yolks, unbeaten
1 tsp. vanilla
2½ cups cake flour, sifted
½ tsp. salt
1 tsp. baking soda
1 cup buttermilk
4 egg whites, stiffly beaten

Melt chocolate in boiling water. Cool. Cream butter and sugar until fluffy. Add egg yolks one at a time and beat well after each addition. Add melted chocolate and vanilla. Mix well.

Sift together flour, salt and soda. Add alternately with buttermilk to chocolate mixture, beating after each addition until smooth. Fold in beaten egg whites. Pour into greased 9" x 13" pan.

Bake in oven at 350 degrees for 30-40 minutes. Cool, frost top with frosting.

Coconut Pecan Frosting

1 cup evaporated milk
1 cup sugar
3 egg yolks
½ cup butter
1 tsp. vanilla extract
1 cup pecans, chopped

Combine the first 5 ingredients in a pan, cook and stir over medium heat until thickened, about 12 minutes.

Add coconut and pecans. Beat until thick enough to spread.

From: **Jack Pandl's
Whitefish Bay Inn**
1319 East Henry Clay Road
Whitefish Bay, Wisconsin

Bread Pudding Toss

¾ *cup sugar*
8 eggs
2 tsps. vanilla extract
1 quart milk

stale bread

½ *cup raisins*
1 cup shredded coconut
cinnamon

Mix first four ingredients together. Into the mixture break as much stale bread, buns, rolls, even rye or whole wheat bread as the mixture will hold. It should be very thick. Add the raisins and coconut and mix well. Pour into greased 9" x 13" pan, spread evenly and sprinkle generously with cinnamon. Bake at 350 degrees for 45 minutes. Remove from oven and cool. With a sharp knife cut into bite-size pieces and mix with whipped topping or whipped cream. Serve. Must be kept refrigerated.

From: **Florena Supper Club**
N3380 Hwy. 13
Medford, Wisconsin

Strawberry Rhubarb Pie

Filling:
7½ cups rhubarb,
　cut in 1" pieces
pinch of salt
½ tsp. nutmeg
2½ cups sugar
3 very heaping Tbsps. flour
2 beaten eggs
1 cup sliced strawberries,
　including juice

Can't Fail Crust:
3 cups flour
1 tsp. salt
1½ cups shortening
1 egg
5 Tbsps. water
1 tsp. vinegar

For crust mix together flour, salt and shortening until it's crumbly like coarse meal. Whip egg, water and vinegar together and add to mealy mixture. Roll out.

Mix pie filling ingredients together, pour into 10" x 1½" deep dish unbaked pie crust. Cover with top crust, pierce top and bake at 350 degrees until bubbling in center, about 1½ hours.

From:　**The Summer Kitchen**
　　　Ephraim, Wisconsin

Raspberry Kuchen

Crust:
¾ cups butter, softened
3 Tbsps. water
1½ cups flour

Custard:
¼ cup flour
1½ cups sugar
pinch of salt
1½ cups sour cream
3 eggs, beaten
1 tsp. vanilla
2 pints raspberries

Mix together ingredients for crust and pat into a 9" x 13" pan.

Combine flour, sugar and salt. Blend in the sour cream, eggs and vanilla. Add the 2 pints of raspberries, rinsed and drained, to the custard mixture. Pour into unbaked crust. Bake at 400 degrees for 30 minutes, turn oven down to 325 degrees and bake another 30 minutes. Sprinkle with the topping for the last 15 minutes of baking.

For the topping mix all ingredients together until crumbly.

Yield: 15 servings.

Topping:
¾ *cup brown sugar*
1½ *cups flour*
¾ *cup white sugar*
¾ *cup butter*

Other fruits that work well with this recipe are:
3 cups fresh sliced peaches
3 cups canned tart cherries, drained
3 cups fresh apples, sliced
3 cups fresh or frozen rhubarb, thawed & drained, diced

From: **Barth's at the Bridge**
N58 W6194 Columbia Road
Cedarburg, Wisconsin

Pumpkin Dessert

Crust:
½ *cup chopped nuts*
1 *box yellow cake mix, without pudding*
½ *cup melted butter*

Filling:
3 *cups canned pumpkin*
1½ *cups sugar*
½ *tsp. salt.*
4 *eggs, beaten*
1 *can evaporated milk*
cinnamon, cloves, ginger
1 *oz. brandy*

Mix together the ingredients for the crust. Reserve 1 cup of mixture for topping. Pat remaining mixture into the bottom of a 9" x 13" pan.

Combine the rest of the ingredients, adding cinnamon, cloves and ginger to taste. Add 1 ounce of brandy. Mix well.

Pour over crust mixture in cake pan and sprinkle reserved mixture over the top. Bake at 375 degrees for 45 minutes or until done. Check with a wooden toothpick inserted in center.

From: **The Star Lake Saloon and Eatery**
Starlake, Wisconsin

Emperor's Torte

4 ozs. semi-sweet chocolate
¾ cup butter
¾ cup sugar
7 egg yolks
1 cup ground almonds
½ tsp. baking powder
7 egg whites

Preheat oven to 350 degrees. Grease and flour sides of two 9" round cake pans. Grease bottom and line with parchment or wax paper. Melt chocolate and cool. Cream sugar and butter together, add the egg yolks to mixture. Add chocolate to mixture and combine thoroughly. Mix almonds with baking powder and add to creamed mixture. Whip the egg whites until stiff. Gently fold into creamed mixture. Divide batter into 2 prepared pans. Bake for 20-25 minutes.

Cool on racks and unmold. Frost with buttercream frosting.

Buttercream Frosting

½ cup butter
1½ cups powdered sugar
½ tsp. vanilla extract
1 Tbsp. warm milk

1 cup chocolate chips
¼ cup butter

1 cup raspberry preserves

Beat the butter till soft. Beat in sugar gradually, adding the vanilla and enough warm milk to make into spreading consistency. Melt the chocolate and butter together.

To assemble, place one chocolate layer on cake plate. Spread chocolate filling over this layer. Place second layer on top of chocolate filling. Spread raspberry preserves on top of this layer.

Frost the sides of the cake with the buttercream frosting. For a decorative touch, pipe lattice design in butterceam on top, then pipe a thicker edge of buttercream around circumference on top of cake and around the bottom of cake.

From the outside the chocolate is not visible, but is a surprise when cut. The entire torte is not very high, maybe 3 inches, because it is a dense, rich cake—to be eaten and savored slowly.

From: **The Sunprint Cafe and Gallery**
638 State Street
Madison, Wisconsin

Waldheim Room Blueberry Pie

5 cups blueberries
4 Tbsps. flour
1 tsp. fresh, ground ginger
1½ cups sugar
1½ tsps. fresh lemon juice

You will need 1 double crust pie shell. Combine sugar, flour, and ginger with berries, then stir in juice.

Fill a 9" pie crust with berry mixture, making a well in the center of pie. Wet edges and cover with top crust. Flute edges, brush with milk, and lightly sprinkle with sugar. Bake 10 minutes at 425 degrees, then 30 minutes more at 350 degrees.

Crust:

3 cups flour
½ tsp. baking powder
¼ tsp. salt
¾ cup lard
½ cup butter
1 egg
1 Tbsp. vinegar
6 Tbsps. water

Cut flour, baking powder, salt, and shortening together. Mix egg and vinegar and add to the flour mixture. Add water 1 tablespoon at a time, only using as much as needed to hold dough in a ball. Makes four 9" crusts.

From: **Hintz's
North Star Lodge**
Starlake, Wisconsin

DESSERTS

Wild Plum Chess Pie

6 cups sugar
3 Tbsps. cornmeal
3 Tbsps. flour

12 eggs
¾ cup milk
1 cup wild plums, pitted and
    ground in food processor
¾ cup melted butter
¾ cup wild plum juice

Combine 3 dry ingredients; combine 5 wet ingredients.

Mix together dry with wet. Bake at 350 degrees for 35-45 minutes in three unbaked pie shells. Yield: 3 pies.

From: **The Old Rittenhouse Inn**
Bayfield, Wisconsin

Bayfield Maple Walnut Pie

1 cup melted butter
2 tsps. salt
12 eggs, beaten
2 cups sugar
4 cups 100% maple syrup
4 cups chopped walnuts

Mix all ingredients together until smooth. Pour into 3 pie shells and bake at 350 degrees until filling is set. Cool and serve with maple ice cream.

From: **The Old Rittenhouse Inn**
Bayfield, Wisconsin

Swedish Apple Pie

8 cups peeled, sliced apples
4 heaping Tbsps. flour
2 cups sour cream
2 eggs, beaten
1 tsp. vanilla extract
¼ tsp. salt
1½ cups sugar
grated rind & juice of 1 lemon

Streusel Topping:
2 cups flour
½ lb. butter, cut in cubes
2 tsps. cinnamon
1 cup sugar

Mix flour, sour cream, eggs, vanilla extract, salt, sugar, lemon rind and juice in a bowl. Stir until smooth. Place 4 cups apples in each 9" pie shell. Pour half of mixture over each pie. Next make the topping by combining all the ingredients in a food processor and processing until it's crumbly. Divide the topping between the two pies. Bake at 350 degrees for 1 hour and 10 minutes or until tiny apple bubbles appear on the top. Smells so good! Yield: two 9" pies.

From: **The Kitchen Table**
East Third & Maple Streets
Marshfield, Wisconsin

Kahlua Pecan Pie

2 ozs. flour
3 cups Karo Light syrup
Kahlua to taste
2 ozs. sugar
8 eggs
3 ozs. butter
8 ozs. pecans

Mix all ingredients together and pour into unbaked pie shells. Bake at 325 degrees for 35 minutes. Yield: 3 pies.

From: **The American Club**
407 Highland Drive
Kohler, Wisconsin

Michael's Bread Pudding

1 cup raisins
3 cups hot water
2 qts. of milk
1 cup sugar
1 tsp. vanilla extract
4 tsps. cinnamon
⅛ tsp. salt
¼ tsp. nutmeg
1 lg. banana, mashed
½ cup honey
12 cups unseasoned croutons
8 large eggs, beaten

Soak raisins in hot water for thirty minutes, drain and set aside. Warm milk, being careful not to scorch. Add sugar, vanilla extract, cinnamon, salt, nutmeg, banana, butter and honey. In a large bowl, mix croutons, milk mixture, raisins and eggs.

Turn into well-greased 9" x 13" baking dish. Bake in a 350 degree oven for 45 minutes. Top individual portions with cream, prepared vanilla pudding, or any favorite dessert sauce. May be frozen and baked at a later date. Yield: 8-12 servings.

From: **Michael's Restaurant**
1815 Ward Avenue
LaCrosse, Wisconsin

Poppy Seed-Marzipan Layer Cake

¾ cup milk, scalded
⅔ cup poppyseeds
¾ cup butter
1 Tbsp. vanilla extract
5 egg yolks
2 cups flour
1 Tbsp. baking powder

Scald the milk, add the poppy seeds. Cool. Cream the butter with the sugar. Add the vanilla. Add the egg yolks, one at a time, mix well. Sift together the flour and baking powder. Add the wet and dry ingredients alternately to the creamed mixture. Beat the egg whites to soft peaks, add sugar and beat

5 egg whites
¼ cup sugar

until stiff. Fold gently into creamed mixture. Bake in two 9″ round pans with greased and floured sides. Line bottoms of pans with wax paper. Bake at 350 degrees for about 30 minutes.

Cool on racks. Split into four layers. Spread with a canned almond (marzipan) filling thinly between layers. Almond filling can also be spread on top of cake or top can be frosted with buttercream.

Buttercream Frosting
for Poppyseed-Marzipan Layer Cake

1 cup butter, soft
1 tsp. almond extract
3 cups powdered sugar
2 Tbsps. warm milk

Beat butter and sugar together, gradually adding almond extract and milk until desired spreading consistency is obtained.

Frost sides of poppy seed cake with buttercream. Top may also be spread with buttercream or with almond filling. Pipe a decorative edge of buttercream around top and bottom of cake. Sides of cake can be covered with slivered almonds. Use whole almonds to decorate the top of the cake.

The basic poppyseed cake can be varied by using raspberry preserves for filling alternate layers, along with the almond filling.

From:

**The Sunprint
Cafe and Gallery**
638 State Street
Madison, Wisconsin

Schwarzwalder Kirschtorte
(German Black Forest Cherry Cake)

2 Tbsps. shortening
6 Tbsps. flour

1 stick unsalted butter
8 eggs
1 tsp. vanilla extract
1 cup sugar
½ cup flour, sifted
½ cup cocoa powder

Grease bottoms and sides of three 8″ cake pans with pastry brush and shortening. Dust each with 2 tablespoons of flour, evenly tipping pans from side to side. Invert pans and tap to remove excess flour. Set aside.

Preheat oven to 325 degrees.

Melt butter. With electric mixer beat eggs, sugar, and vanilla at high speed until fluffy and thick (10-15 minutes.)

Sift together ½ cup of flour and cocoa. sprinkle a little at a time over the egg mixture gently folding it with a rubber spatula. Fold in melted butter a tablespoon at a time. Do not overmix. Bake on middle rack of oven for 12-15 minutes or until cake tester or toothpick comes out clean when inserted in center of cake. Remove cakes from oven and let cool for 5 minutes in pans. Run sharp knife around edge of cakes and turn them onto racks to cool completely.

Syrup:
¾ cup sugar
⅓ cup Kirsch
1 cup water

Combine water and sugar in a small saucepan over medium heat and bring to a boil. Stir until sugar is dissolved. Let cool and add Kirsch.

Put cakes on large baking sheet. Prick each layer lightly in several places with a fork. Sprinkle each layer evenly with syrup and let set for 10 minutes.

Filling:
¾ of 1 16-oz. can red, tart
  pitted cherries
1 pinch ground cloves
3 Tbsps. sugar
3 Tbsps. cornstarch

Take three-quarters of a 16-ounce can of red, tart, pitted cherries and juice and pour into a small saucepan. Add sugar and pinch of cloves. Bring to a boil and remove from heat. Dissolve cornstarch in 2 tablespoons cold water. Stir into hot cherries and put

back on heat. Stir until it's back to a boil and thickened. Remove from heat. Let cool to room temperature.

Topping:
3 cups chilled heavy cream,
not "whipping" cream
½ tsp. vanilla extract
½ cup powdered sugar
2 ozs. Kirsch

In chilled mixing bowl beat heavy cream until lightly thickened. Sift in powdered sugar. Continue beating until cream forms firm peaks on beater when lifted out of bowl. Pour in slowly the 2 ounces of Kirsch and ½ teaspoon of the vanilla extract, beating only until both are absorbed into the cream.

Assemble the cake on a round serving platter. Place the first layer in the center. Cover with the cherry filling. Make sure it doesn't run down the sides. Place in the refrigerator for 15 minutes to set. Now place the second layer on top and spread ½ inch of whipped cream on top of that with a spatula. Then set the third layer in place. Spread the top and sides of the cake with the remaining cream.

Decorate the cake with the leftover cherries, or if you prefer, Maraschino cherries and shaved chocolate. Set back in refrigerator to set. It is now ready to serve.

From: **Bernard's
Continental Restaurant**
North Second Street
Stevens Point, Wisconsin

Burnt Cream

1 pt. whipping cream
4 egg yolks
½ cup sugar
1 Tbsp. vanilla extract
sugar for topping

Preheat oven to 350 degrees. Heat cream over low heat until bubbles form around edge of pan. Beat egg yolks and sugar together until thick, about 3 minutes. Gradually beat cream into the egg yolks. Stir in vanilla and pour into six 6-ounce custard cups. Place custard cups in baking pan that has about ½ inch of water in the bottom. Bake until set, about 45 minutes. Remove custard cups from water and refrigerate until chilled. Sprinkle each custard with about 2 teaspoons of sugar. Place on top rack under broiler and cook until topping is medium brown. Chill before serving.

From: **Michael's Restaurant**
1815 Ward Avenue
LaCrosse, Wisconsin

Mardi Gras Frappe a la Maison

1 cup diced cantaloupe
1 cup diced catawba
1 cup diced honeydew

½ cup German white wine
   (Spatelese)
½ cup sugar
¼ cup fresh lime juice
¼ cup fresh lemon juice
3 Tbsps. honey

½ pint fresh blackberries
½ pint fresh blueberries
2 Tbsps. fresh lemon juice
1 cup brut Champagne
½ pint fresh raspberries
¼ cup sugar
3 ozs. Kirschwasser
½ cup ginger ale

Puree the melon in a food processor or blender until velvety smooth.

Add the wine, lemon, lime juices, sugar and honey to the melon. Stir by hand until thoroughly combined. Freeze mixture until consistency is that of sherbet.

Marinate berries in mixture of sugar, lemon juice, Kirschwasser, Champagne and ginger ale for 1 hour.

To serve, place one large scoop of fresh melon into a wide rimmed champagne glass. Ladle 4 ounces of berries over the melon. Garnish with a dollop of whipped cream and a mint sprig.

From: **Karl Ratzsch's**
          320 East Mason Street
          Milwaukee, Wisconsin

Frozen Pear Souffle
with
Seckel Pears Poached in Red Wine
Strawberry Sauce and Creme Anglaise

6 small Seckel pears,
peeled, halved and cored
Red wine to cover
½ cup sugar

6 egg yolks
2½ ozs. sugar
2 ozs. Pear William
4 reserved pear halves,
pureed, about ¼ cup
2 egg whites, 1 oz. sugar
whipped to soft peaks
½ cup heavy cream, whipped

Bring pears, wine and sugar to simmer and cook until pears are tender when pierced with a skewer. Cool pears and liquid.

In a double boiler, whip the egg yolks, sugar and liqueur to a ribbon stage. Do not overcook. Cool mixture. Fold in pureed pears, egg whites and heavy cream. Put in molds and freeze.

Strawberry Sauce:
Clean and hull 1 pint of strawberries and put in food processor. Add cold liquid from pears until desired consistency. (About ¼ cup liquid to 1 pint strawberries.)

Creme Anglaise:
2 cups milk
4 ozs. sugar
6 egg yolks, whipped
½ vanilla bean, split

Bring milk and one-half sugar to a boil. Slowly add the rest of the sugar and egg yolks to mixture. Put mixture back on stove and cook until the cream coats the back of a spoon. Do not overcook. Strain and cool.

To set up, unmold the pear souffle in the center of plate. Place 2 thinly sliced Seckel pears on each side of the souffle. Alternately ladle strawberry sauce and creme anglaise over all.

From: **John Byron's**
777 E. Michigan Avenue
Galleria Level
Milwaukee, Wisconsin

Chocolate Steamed Pudding

1 Tbsp. butter
1½ ozs. unsweetened chocolate
1 egg
1 cup sugar
½ tsp. vanilla extract
1 cup coffee, cooled
1½ cups flour, sifted
¼ tsp. salt
1½ tsps. baking powder

In a double boiler or over very low heat, melt butter and chocolate, set side to cool.

Beat egg and sugar together, add vanilla and beat again. Add chocolate mixture, and mix again. Add cooled coffee, blend well. Sift dry ingredients together and add. Batter should be smooth. Butter eight 6-ounce custard cups. Using a level 4-ounce ladle, fill cups with chocolate mixture. Cover each cup tightly with foil.

Set cups in deep baking pan. Add ½" hot water to baking pan. Cover pan with foil and preheated 350 degree oven for 30 minutes. Cool slightly before unmolding. Serve warm with "Ellie's Mom's Sauce."

Ellie's Mom's Sauce

2½ cups sifted, powdered sugar
2 eggs
¼ lb. + 2 Tbsps. butter
¼ tsp. salt
1½ tsps. vanilla extract
1 cup whipping cream

Chill large mixing bowl and whip in freezer.

Combine first 5 ingredients in another bowl and mix until creamy and smooth.

Add whipping cream to chilled bowl and beat until slightly thickened. continue to beat with chilled whip and slowly fold in egg mixture, maintaining as much air as possible in the cream. Whip by hand until smooth. Yield: 3 cups sauce.

From: **Quivey's Grove**
6261 Nesbit Road
Madison, Wisconsin

Tarte au Citron

Pastry:
1½ cups flour
⅓ cup butter
⅓ cup sugar
¼ tsp. salt
3 egg yolks
1 tsp. vanilla extract

Filling:
3 eggs
¾ cup sugar
2 lemons, juice & rind
⅓ cup melted butter
1 cup ground, blanched almonds

For the pastry, make a well in flour, add butter, egg yolks, sugar and vanilla. Mix until blended. Chill 30 minutes.

Roll out the dough, line 9" flan pan with it and chill until firm. Line the dough with wax paper, pressing it well into the edges, fill with uncooked beans and bake in a preheated oven for 10-12 minutes or until the pastry is set. Remove the paper and beans and bake the shell 3-5 minutes more, until the bottom is no longer soft.

Beat eggs and sugar until light and thick enough to leave a ribbon trail when the whisk is lifted. Stir in lemon juice and rind, followed by the melted butter and ground almonds.

Pour the mixture in the pie shell and bake in a preheated oven for 350 degrees for 25-30 minutes or until the filling is set. Serve the pie at room temperature.

From: **Ovens of Brittany
—East**
1718 Fordem Road
Madison, Wisconsin

Chocolate Mousse

1½ tsps. unflavored gelatin
2 Tbsps. cold water
1 cup whole milk
2 1-oz. squares unsweetened
   chocolate, shaved

Mix gelatin and water until dissolved. Place milk in saucepan and scald. Add chocolate shavings. Stir to dissolve. Blend in gelatin. Remove from heat. Add sugar, salt, mix well. Allow to cool slightly and stir in vanilla. Fold

¾ cup sugar
½ tsp. salt
1 tsp. vanilla extract
2 cups whipped cream

whipped cream into chocolate mixture and turn into 9" x 12" pan and chill until firm.

Turn finished mousse into large stemmed glasses. Garnish with cream and shaved sweet chocolate.

From: **The Fox and Hounds**
1298 Freiss Lake Road
Hubertus, Wisconsin

Chocolate Pie Royale

⅓ cup egg whites
1 tsp. vinegar
1⅓ cups sugar
½ tsp. cinnamon

Filling:
1⅓ cups chocolate chips
3 egg yolks
⅓ cup sugar
⅓ cup water
3 cups whipping cream

Butter 9" pie plate. Beat egg whites until stiff. Add vinegar and cinnamon. Then gradually add sugar. Continue to beat until all sugar is blended and mixture forms stiff peaks. Spread batter over bottom and sides of pie plate. Bake at 250 degrees for 1 hour. Turn off oven. Let shell dry in oven overnight.

For filling melt chocolate chips in top of double boiler. Spread about 2 tablespoons of melted chocolate on bottom and sides of shell. Combine egg yolks, sugar, and water with remaining chocolate and cook until thick. Cool. Whip cream until stiff. Spread 1 layer of whipped cream over chocolate layer. Then combine remaining chocolate mixture with whipped cream. Pile mixture over cream. Refrigerate until well set. Yield: 10-12 servings.

From: **Boder's on the River**
11919 N. River Road
Mequon, Wisconsin

Turtle Pie

¼ cup cream
¾ cup brown sugar
2 Tbsps. melted butter
6 Tbsps. corn syrup
1 cup pecans, chopped
1 9" pie shell
1½ tsps. sugar
1½ tsps. cornstarch
¼ tsp. salt
¾ tsp. gelatin
2 egg yolks
¼ cup milk
¾ cup melted chocolate chips
½ pt. whipped cream

Combine first 4 ingredients, cook until 227 degrees on a candy thermometer. Add pecans, pour into pie shell. Cool. In saucepan mix next 4 ingredients. Add egg yolks, mix till smooth. Add milk, stirring constantly over moderate heat till it's 160 degrees. Remove from heat, mix in melted chocolate chips. Cool. Fold in whipped cream. Pour over candy layer. Drizzle with melted chocolate and decorate with pecans.

From: **Quivey's Grove**
6261 Nesbit Road
Madison, Wisconsin

Inns & Restaurants

The numbers inside the parentheses (   ) after the name of the restaurant indicate the pages on which recipes from that restaurant appear. Unless otherwise specified reservations are not necessary.

MADISON

The Cafe Palms
536 West Washington Avenue
Madison, Wis. 53703
608/256-0166
(21, 89, 95)

Chez Michel
7601 Mineral Point Road
Madison, Wis. 53719
608/833-6969   Reservations advisable
(31, 93)

L'Etoile
25 N. Pinckney
Madison, Wis. 53703
608/251-0500   Reservations necessary
(33, 84)

The Fess Hotel
123 Doty Street
Madison, Wis. 53703
608/256-0263   Reservations advisable
(25, 78, 89)

The Ovens of Brittany—East
1718 Fordem Road
Madison, Wis. 53704
608/241-7779   Reservations advisable
(10, 13, 23, 48, 87, 120)

The Ovens of Brittany—Monroe Street
1831 Monroe Street
Madison, Wis. 53705
608/251-2119   Reservations advisable
(51, 57, 68)

Quivey's Grove
6261 Nesbit Road
Madison, Wis. 53713
608/273-4900   Reservations advisable
(21, 38, 47, 67, 73, 96, 119, 122)

The Stockpot
1730 Fordem Road
Madison, Wis. 53704
608/241-2924
(91)
(As we went to press the Stockpot discontinued serving luncheon. Food available on take-out basis.)

The Sunprint Cafe and Gallery
638 State Street
Madison, Wis. 53703
608/255-1555
(94, 108, 112)

MILWAUKEE

Chip and Py's
815 South 5th Street
Milwaukee, Wis. 53204
414/645-3435
(41)

Cracovia Restaurant
1531 West Lincoln Avenue
Milwaukee, Wis. 53215
414/383-8688
(49, 66)

Grenadier's
747 North Broadway
Milwaukee, Wis. 53202
414/276-0747   Reservations necessary
(81)

John Byron's
777 E. Michigan Avenue, Galleria Level
Milwaukee, Wis. 53201
414/291-5220   Reservations advisable
(34, 43, 58, 118)

INNS & RESTAURANTS

Karl Ratzsch's
320 East Mason Street
Milwaukee, Wis. 53202
414/276-2720
(45, 55, 60, 83, 117)

Mader's
1037 North Third Street
Milwaukee, Wis. 53203
414/271-3377
(65, 71)

SOUTHEASTERN WISCONSIN

Barth's at the Bridge
N58 W6194 Columbia Road
Cedarburg, Wis. 53012
414/377-0660   Reservations advisable
(49, 68, 69, 106)

Boder's on the River
11919 N. River Road W43
Mequon, Wis. 53092
414/242-0335
(121)

The Fox and Hounds
1298 Freiss Lake Road
Hubertus, Wis. 53033
414/251-4100   Reservations advisable
(64, 92, 120)

The Golden Mast Inn
1270 Lacy's Lane
Okauchee, Wis. 53069
414/567-7047   Reservations advisable
(52, 74, 97)

Inn of the Four Seasons
Hwy. 99 and County E
Eagle, Wis. 53119
414/594-3318   Reservations advisable
(26, 96)

Jack Pandl's Whitefish Bay Inn
1319 East Henry Clay Road
Whitefish Bay, Wis. 53217
414/964-3800
(5, 50, 104)

The Red Geranium
Hwy. 50E
Lake Geneva, Wis. 53147
414/248-3637
(56, 70, 94)

Timmer's on Big Cedar Lake
5151 Timmer's Bay Drive
West Bend, Wis. 53095
414/338-8666
(14)

DOOR COUNTY

Bailey's Harbor Yacht Club
Bailey's Harbor, Wis. 54202
414/839-2336   Reservations advisable
(72, 78)

**Faller's Seafood Restaurant at
The Renaissance Inn**
414 Maple Drive
Sister Bay, Wis. 53234
414/854-5107   Reservations advisable
(34, 36, 79)

The Summer Kitchen
Ephraim, Wis. 54211
(4, 6, 8, 106)

The White Gull Inn
Fish Creek, Wis. 54212
414/868-3517   Reservations advisable
(22, 44, 103)

AT LARGE

The American Club
407 Highland Drive
Kohler, Wis. 53044
414/457-8000   Reservations necessary
(41, 111)

Bernard's Continental Restaurant
North Second Street
Stevens Point, Wis. 54481
715/344-3365   Reservations advisable
(62, 93, 114)

The Blue Bayou Inn
Manitowish Waters, Wis. 54545
715/543-2537
(30, 82)

Carver's on the Lake
99 Inlet Road
Green Lake, Wis. 54941
414/294-6931   Reservations advisable
(32, 77, 95)

The Duke House
Mineral Point, Wis. 53565
608/987-2821
Bed & Breakfast
(20, 22, 27)

Morena Supper Club
3380 Hwy. 13
Medford, Wis. 54451
715/749-2866
(42, 72, 105)

The Granary
0 West 6th Avenue
Oshkosh, Wis. 54901
414/233-3929   Reservations advisable
(0)

Kintz's North Star Lodge
Starlake, Wis. 54561
715/542-3600
(4, 109)

The Jamieson House
Poynette, Wis. 53955
608/635-4100   Reservations requested
(37, 70, 101)

The Kitchen Table
East Third & Maple Streets
Marshfield, Wis. 54449
(42, 46, 111)

Keffel's Supper Club
319 Forest Avenue
Antigo, Wis. 54409
715/627-7027
(5, 46)

Michael's Restaurant
1815 Ward Avenue
LaCrosse, Wis. 54601
608/788-1900   Reservations advisable
(56, 82, 88, 112, 116)

The Mill Road Cafe
Mill Road
Galesville, Wis. 54360
(7, 20, 102)

The Old Rittenhouse Inn
Bayfield, Wis. 54814
715/779-5765   Reservations necessary
(110)

Peck's Plantation
Hwy. 73 East
Wautoma, Wis. 54982
715/787-3301
(9, 11)

The Prairieland Cafe
137 Albany Street
Spring Green, Wis. 53588
(12)

The Red Rooster Cafe
Mineral Point, Wis. 53565
(6)

The Round Barn
Hwy. 14 East
Spring Green, Wis. 53588
(25)

The Star Lake Saloon and Eatery
Starlake, Wis. 54561
(19, 88, 97, 107)

Sunrise Lodge
Land O'Lakes, Wis. 54540
715/547-3674
(3, 31)

The Vintage House
Hwy. 13 North
Wisconsin Rapids, Wis. 54494
715/421-4900   Reservations advisable
(24, 61, 90)

Index

A

Abelskivers 4
Almond—
  Soup, Cream of 41
Appetizers 29-36
  Borek 37
  Clams Renaissance 34
  Cranberry Frost................... 31
  Leek & Chevre Tart 33
  Morel Tart 31
  Quenelles of Scallops 34
  Seafood Sausage 32
  Seafood Triangles................. 36
  Smoked Trout Puffs................ 38
Apples—
  in Abelskivers 4
  Bombay Salad 89
  Swedish Pie 111
Apricot—
  Puffs 25
Asparagus—
  Soup, Cream of 41
Autumn Salad...................... 93

B

Bacon—
  Hot Dressing 97
Basil—
  Sweet Shrimp...................... 82
Bayou Crawfish Etoufee 80
Beef—
  Braised Roll-Up 66
  Hungarian Goulash 65
  Tenderloin Madeira 68
  Tenderloin Spinach Salad 90
  Wellington 68
Bernard's House Dressing 93
Black Bean—
  Southern, Soup 49
Blueberries—
  Coffeecake........................ 22
  in Pancakes 3
  Mardi Gras Frappe 117
  Waldheim Room Pie 109
Bombay Salad...................... 89
Borek 37

Bread—
  Anise 24
  Baking Powder Biscuits 19
  Pudding, Michael's 112
  Pudding, Toss 105
  Orange Nut Loaf 25
  Spicy Apple Cinnamon 24
  Walnut Whole Wheat 26
Broccoli—
  and Mushroom Soup, Cream of 42
  Fresh Vegetables in Puff Pastry 14
  in Garden Vegetable Dish 14
Brunch.......................... 1-16
Burnt Cream 116
Buttercream—
  Frosting 108
  Frosting for
    Poppy Seed-Marzipan Cake...... 113
Buttermilk—
  Pancakes 3

C

Cajun Barbecued Shrimp 79
Cake—
  German Sweet Chocolate 104
  Mississippi Mud 102
  Poppy Seed-Marzipan 112
Calvados—
  Cream Sauce 67
Cauliflower—
  Fresh Vegetables in Puff Pastry 14
  Soup, Cream of 42
Cheddar Cheese Dressing 96
Chicken—
  Almond Soup 44
  Curried Salad 89
  Deviled 56
  Pappas Stuffed Breast............. 56
  Richelieu 57
  Stuffed Breast 55
Chocolate—
  Emperor's Torte 108
  Cake, German Sweet 104
  Mississippi Mud Cake 102
  Mousse........................... 120
  Pie Royale 120
  Steamed Pudding 119

Ciociara Sauce 10
Citron—
   Tarte au 120
Coconut Pecan Frosting 104
Coffeecake—
   Blueberry......................... 22
   Nut Roll 27
   Peaches & Cream 23
Cole Slaw—
   Oriental 88
   Saloon 88
Cranberry Frost 31
Cream—
   Burnt............................ 116
   of, see Soups 39
   Salmon with Morels & 84
Creme Anglaise 118
Crawfish—
   Bayou Etoufee 80
Cucumber Yogurt Dressing 94

D

Desserts—
   Bayfield Maple Walnut Pie........ 110
   Bread Pudding Toss 105
   Burnt Cream..................... 116
   Chocolate Mousse 120
   Chocolate Pie Royale 121
   Chocolate Steamed Pudding 119
   Emperor's Torte 108
   Frozen Pear Souffle 118
   German Sweet Chocolate Cake 104
   Kahlua Pecan Pie 111
   Mardi Gras Frappe 117
   Michael's Bread Pudding 112
   Mississippi Mud Cake............ 102
   Poppy Seed-Marzipan
      Layer Cake 112
   Poppy Seed Torte 103
   Pumpkin Dessert 107
   Raspberry Kuchen 106
   Schwarzwalder Kirschtorte 114
   Strawberry Rhubarb Pie 106
   Strawberry Wafer Torte 101
   Swedish Apple Pie 111
   Tarte au Citron 120
   Turtle Pie....................... 122
   Waldheim Room Blueberry Pie 109
   Wild Plum Chess Pie 110
Deviled Chicken 56

Dill—
   Pickle Soup...................... 49
   Tomato, Soup.................... 51
Dijon—
   Lemon Dressing 96
   in Deviled Chicken 56
Dijonnaise—
   Swordfish 81
Dressings—
   Bernard's House 93
   Cheddar Cheese 96
   Cucumber Yogurt 94
   French Dressing 97
   Ginger Vinaigrette 94
   Hot Bacon 97
   Lemon Dijon..................... 96
   Raspberry Vinaigrette 95
   Tarragon and Mustard Vinaigrette .. 95
   Vinaigrette, Stockpot 91

E

Eggs—
   Kitchen Scrambler................ 8
Ellie's Mom's Sauce 119
Emperor's Torte 108
Etoufee—
   Bayou Crawfish 80

F

Fish—
   Crawfish, Bayou Etoufee 80
   Salmon—
      with Morels and Cream 84
      Poached, with
         Mousseline Sauce 77
      Steak, Grilled Choron 83
Frappe—
   Mardi Gras, a la Maison 117
Frosting—
   Buttercream 108
   Buttercream for Poppy Seed-
      Marzipan Layer Cake........... 113
   Coconut Pecan 104

G

Garden Vegetable Dish............. 14
Garided Tourkolimano 82
German—
   Black Forest Cherry Cake 114

Pancake 5
Sweet Chocolate Cake 104
Goose—
Roast Breast of 64
Goulash—
Hungarian 65
Green Peppercorn—
Cream Sauce with, ... 70
Gulf Shrimp Maureen 78

H

Hungarian Goulash 65

K

Kahlua—
Pecan Pie 111
Kirschtorte—
Schwarzwalder 114
Kuchen—
Raspberry 106

L

Lamb—
Marinade for 70
Leek—
and Chevre Tart 33
and Shrimp Soup 43
Lemon—
Dijon Dressing 96
Citron, Tarte au 120
Liver Dumpling Soup 50

M

Madeira—
Sauce 69
Tenderloin 68
Maple—
Bayfield Walnut Pie 110
Mardi Gras Frappe a la Maison 117
Marinade—
for Lamb 70
Marinated—
Mushroom Salad 92
Vegetable Salad 87
Meat and Poultry—
  Beef—
    Braised Roll-Up 66
    Hungarian Goulash 65

Tenderloin Madeira 68
Tenderloin Spinach Salad 90
Wellington 68
Lamb—
Marinade for 70
Pork Fremont 67
Veal—
Escalope de 72
Morels, with 73
Ragout Soup 52
Scallopini 72
Schnitzel—
  Count Esterhazy 71
  Wiener 74
  Wiener Emmanthal 74
Tenderloin Medallions with
  Green Peppercorn Sauce 70
Mississippi Mud Cake 102
Moussaka 12
Morels—
Sauce for Veal 73
Salmon with 84
Tart 31
Muffins—
Bran 20
Infamous Fruit and Honey Bran 20
Pumpkin 21
Raspberry 21
Mushroom—
Broccoli and, Soup 42
Marinated Salad 92
Soup, Cream of 54
Wild Rice, Pea and, Salad 91

O

Oriental Cole Slaw 88

P

Pancakes—
Buttermilk 3
German 5
Potato Zucchini 13
Pasty—
Cornish 6
Pear—
Autumn Salad 93
Frozen Souffle 118
Pecan—
Coconut Frosting 104
Kahlua, Pie 111

Pesto—
Pasta 10
Pie—
Bayfield Maple Walnut 110
Chocolate Royale 121
Kahlua Pecan..................... 111
Strawberry Rhubarb 106
Swedish Apple 111
Turtle 122
Waldheim Room Blueberry 109
Wild Plum Chess 110
Pie Crust—
Cornish Pasty 6
Swedish Apple 111
Tarte au Citron 120
Waldheim Room Blueberry 109
Plum—
Wild Chess Pie................... 110
Poppy Seed—
Marzipan Layer Cake 112
Torte 103
Potato—
Cheese Soup 46
Cucumber Soup 46
Duchesse........................ 79
Sweet, Bernard's 63
Zucchini, Pancakes 13
Pork Fremont 67
Poultry—
Chicken—
Almond Soup 44
Deviled 56
Pappas Stuffed Breast........... 56
Richelieu 57
Stuffed Breast 55
Duckling—
a l'Orange 62
Chasseur 61
Croustade of................... 58
Salmi a la Ratzsch 60
Goose—
Roast Breast of 64
Pudding—
Bread, Michael's 112
Bread, Toss 105
Chocolate, Steamed............. 119
Pumpkin—
Dessert........................ 107
Muffins 121

Q

Quenelles of Scallops 34
Quiche—
Mexican 7

R

Raspberry—
Kuchen......................... 106
Muffins 21
Vinaigrette 95
Ravioli 9
Rhubarb—
Strawberry Pie 106

S

Salads—
Autumn 93
Bombay 89
Chicken, Curried 89
Cole Slaw—
Oriental 88
Saloon 88
Mushroom, Marinated 92
Tenderloin Spinach 90
Vegetable, Marinated.......... 87
Wild Rice, Pea and Mushroom 91
Salad Dressings—
see Dressings—
Sandwich—
HiFi 6
Scallops—
Coquilles St. Jacques
Parisienne..................... 78
Quenelles 34
Schwarzwalder Kirschtorte 114
Scones—
Highland Oat 22
Seafood—
Ciociara Sauce................. 10
Sausage 32
Triangles 36
see Shrimp—
Shishkebab—
Lamb, Marinade for 70
Shrimp—
Cajun Barbecued 79
Garided Tourkolimano 82

Gulf Maureen 78
Leek and, Soup 43
Sweet Basil 82
Soups—
  Cream—
    Almond......................... 41
    Asparagus 41
    Broccoli and Mushroom 42
    Cauliflower 42
    Chicken Almond 44
    Leek and Shrimp 43
    Mushroom...................... 45
    Potato Cheese 46
    Potato Cucumber 46
    Sausage, Cheese and Beer 47
    Vegetable 48
  Dill Pickle 49
  Liver Dumpling 50
  Southern Black Bean 49
  Tomato Dill..................... 51
  Veal Ragout..................... 52
Spaghetti Sauce 11
Strawberry—
  Rhubarb Pie 106
  Wafer Torte..................... 101
  Sauce—118
Streusel—
  Peaches and Cream Coffeecake..... 23
  Swedish Apple Pie 111
Swedish Apple Pie 111
Sweet—
  Basil Shrimp 82
  Potato, Bernard's 63
Swordfish Dijonnaise 81

T

Tenderloin—
  Madeira 68
  Spinach Salad 90
  Veal, Medallions of............... 70
Tomato—
  Dill Soup 51
Torte—
  Emperor's 108
  Poppy Seed 103
  Schwarzwalder Kirsch 114
  Strawberry Wafer 101
Tourkolimano—
  Garided........................ 82

V

Veal—
  Escalope de 72
  Morels, with 73
  Ragout Soup.................... 52
  Scallopini 72
  Schnitzel—
    Count Esterhazy............... 71
    Wiener 74
    Wiener Emmanthal 74
  Tenderloin Medallions with
    Green Peppercorn Sauce 70
Vegetables—
  Fresh, in Puff Pastry 14
  Garden Dish 14
  Marinated, Salad 87
  Soup, Cream of 48
Vinaigrette—
  Ginger.......................... 94
  Raspberry 95
  Stockpot 91
  Tarragon and Mustard 95

W

Walnut—
  Bayfield Maple Pie 110
Wellington—
  Beef 68
Wild Rice—
  Dressing 15
  Pea and Mushroom Salad 91

Y

Yogurt—
  in Bombay Salad 89
  Cucumber Dressing.............. 94

Z

Zucchini—
  Potato Pancakes 13